West Virginia

MOUNTAIN MAJESTY

West Virginia

MOUNTAIN MAJESTY

James E. Casto, Writer

Gerald S. Ratliff, Chief Photographer

Anne H. Crozier, Designer

Published by Publications Management Associates, Inc.
P. O. Drawer 41309
4009 Brookhaven Drive
Nashville, Tennessee 37204
(615)298-1498 Fax (615)386-3955

in cooperation with
the West Virginia Division of Culture and History
Charleston, West Virginia

design and layout by
A. C. Designs
Charleston, West Virginia

First edition, first printing
Printed in the United States of America
ISBN 0-9651580-0-4

MICHAEL KELLER

Distributed by the West Virginia Division of Culture and History, The Cultural Center, 1900 Kanawha Boulevard East, Charleston, WV 25305; phone (304)558-0220, fax (304)558-2779.

Contents

©VAN SLIDER

Wintertime in Mineral County

Acknowledgments

Many people and organizations contributed to the making of *West Virginia: Mountain Majesty*. They include Ken Sullivan, our editor and also editor of *Goldenseal*, the quarterly magazine of West Virginia traditional life published by the West Virginia Division of Culture and History. *Goldenseal* contributed photographs and much staff time to the project, including that of Cornelia Alexander and Debby Sonis Jackson.

Commissioner Bill Drennen of the Division of Culture and History was deeply involved in the project from start to finish, working closely with the editor and with publisher Ray Lawson. Deputy Commissioner Bill Farrar also contributed, as critic and photographer, and Director Fred Armstrong of the Archives and History Section participated in planning the book and reviewed Jim Casto's draft manuscript. The contribution of the Archives was essential, as evidenced by the large number of their photos appearing in the following pages, with staffers Greg Clark and Debra Basham especially helpful.

A long list of photographers contributed to the project, working under the direction of chief photographer Gerald Ratliff. They include West Virginia Division of Tourism photographers Dave Fattaleh and Steve Shaluta, as well as Mike Keller at Culture and History. The other photographers were Van Slider, who contributed the cover and other photographs, Rick Lee, Todd Hanson, the late George J. Kossuth, Larry Belcher, Peggy Powell, Larry Pierce, Brian Blauser, Greg Henshaw, Steve Payne and Melvin Grubb.

We appreciate the cooperation of *Wonderful West Virginia* magazine, Editor Nancy Clark and photographer Ron Snow in particular. We thank the *Huntington Herald-Dispatch*, Tim Hensley, and the West Virginia and Regional History Collection at West Virginia University for generously contributing photographs.

We especially thank Governor Gaston Caperton and his staff for their enthusiastic support of this project. They were instrumental in conveying the importance of corporate participation to the businesses who made this publication possible.

And finally, our thanks to those businesses whose names and stories you will find in the corporate profile section. They are the backbone of West Virginia's economy, past and future. We are grateful that they have shared their history and their resources.

Right: The redbud brings spring to Brandywine.

GERALD S. RATLIFF

Governor's Foreword

West Virginia is a proud state, teeming with America's most dedicated and hard-working people. Out of our majestic mountains, we have cultivated a thriving business economy in the midst of nature's splendid beauty. With a work force full of hope for the future and renowned for its compassion, commitment, honesty and humility, West Virginia is a success story in the making.

The Mountain State always has been a frontier land. It was a wilderness frontier in 1716 when Colonel Alexander Spotswood said, "Thus it was decided to cross the mountains," and continues today to be a frontier for education, health care and telecommunications technology. While we cherish our humble beginnings, West Virginians are looking to the future with excitement and fortitude.

The nation's lowest crime rate, a nationally heralded education system that includes 16,000 computers in elementary schools, excellent medical facilities, one of the first states to be designated a "clean state," unsurpassed telecommunications capabilities and a booming tourism industry have transformed West Virginia from a state lauded for its unparalleled beauty to one that also is recognized for its diverse economic opportunities.

From our rugged woodlands and clear mountain streams to our flourishing business and industry, the following pages highlight West Virginia's secret to success and our confidence in the future.

Welcome to West Virginia. Explore our state and discover its magic.

Gaston Caperton, Governor

Right: Historic railroad bridge in Fayette County.

TODD A HANSON

Introduction

S ooner or later, it happens to nearly every West Virginian. You're away from home. In New York or maybe California or perhaps Hong Kong. You're making small talk with somebody when the conversation turns homeward, and you're asked: "Where are you from?"

"West Virginia," you say.

"Oh, that's nice," comes the reply. "I have a cousin who lives in Richmond. Maybe you know him."

To those of us who call West Virginia home, this is a source of aggravation. How can so many people not know that West Virginia and Virginia are two separate — and vastly different — states?

Even worse, too many other people think they know all about West Virginia, but have in mind a clichéd stereotype based largely on the inaccurate fashion in which our state is sometimes portrayed in the media. If all you know about West Virginia is what you've seen on television or at the movies, in comic strips and even the pages of such a respected publication as *The Washington Post*, then you're apt to think it's a state populated exclusively by first cousins of the "Beverly Hillbillies" and a hopeless backwater.

Autumn brings the richness of its colors to a Monongalia County farm.

First-time visitors sometimes seem genuinely surprised at what they discover here.

In truth, those who don't know that there is a West Virginia and those condescending souls inclined to look down on the state as some sort of poor relation are more to be pitied than scorned.

They don't know what a unique and wonderful place our state is.

And that's what this book is all about.

This is not a history book, although there's a great deal of West Virginia's remarkable history in it. Nor is it a travel guide, though I hope some readers, after taking an

Left - A young skier takes it over the top at Snowshoe Resort in Pocahontas County.

armchair tour in these pages, will be encouraged to get in their cars and hit the road, exploring our state firsthand.

Not a history, not a travel guide, but a celebration — a word-and-picture look at some of the people, places, things and events that make West Virginia the special place it is.

West Virginia is 24,232 square miles of mountains and valleys, forests and fields, caves and creeks, rural vistas and busy cities.

GERALD S. RATLIFF

Spruce Knob, West Virginia's highest mountain, gets some of the state's deepest snow.

West Virginia is a summer kissed by fresh mountain air, a fall that's a kaleidoscope of blazing red and gold, a winter that's landscapes blanketed in snow, a spring that's dogwood, redbud, wildflowers and song birds. Almost Heaven, a hit song called it, and we don't disagree.

West Virginia is banjos, fiddles, backporch music and patchwork quilts — along with symphonies and jazz, outdoor dramas, moonlight concerts and museums.

West Virginia is the hands of a potter shaping clay, the hands of a glassblower transforming the most basic raw materials into a thing of beauty — and the hands of a skilled computer operator at the FBI's futuristic new fingerprint identification center.

West Virginia is world-class whitewater and golf at championship courses. It's hunting, fishing, camping, hiking, biking, rock climbing, skiing, horseback riding and, yes, even scuba-diving in the crystal clear waters of Summersville Lake.

West Virginia is a year-round calendar of fairs and festivals. Pick a weekend, any weekend, and somewhere in the state there's fun going on. And you're invited.

West Virginia is Harper's Ferry, the scene of John Brown's famous raid, and Blennerhassett Island, where Aaron Burr plotted empire until Thomas Jefferson caught

on. It's the historic houses once frequented by Stonewall Jackson, Booker T. Washington and Pearl Buck. It's the steel mills of the Northern Panhandle, the chemical plants of the Kanawha Valley and the tipples that guard the steep hills of the southern coal fields.

STEPHEN J. SHALUTA, JR.

Fishermen work the quiet waters of Watoga State Park.

West Virginia is the cry of "All Aboard" as a chugging Shay locomotive starts another run at the Cass Scenic Railroad. It's the silent, relentless search of the stars at the

National Radio Astronomy Observatory at Green Bank. And it's the Mennonite farmers raising families in the old, simple, good ways — within sight of the space-age dishes of the radio astronomers.

West Virginia is a stroll in Huntington's scenic Ritter Park, a visit to Charleston's Sternwheel Regatta or a trip to Helvetia, where that small community's residents work hard to keep their Swiss heritage alive.

West Virginia is famous sons and daughters — like Senator Robert C. Byrd, bold Chuck Yeager, and country music star Kathy Mattea.

West Virginia is all this and more. Much more.

So the biggest challenge in putting together this volume wasn't figuring out what to put in, it was deciding — often with a real sense of regret — what to leave out. We began by drawing up a long list of things to be included, then as the work unfolded, we found ourselves forced to start picking and choosing. Some may disagree with our decisions. But this is not meant to be a West Virginia encyclopedia, but rather a sampler.

We hope that readers, after enjoying this book, will be prompted to go to their nearest bookstore or library and search the shelves for more information about West Virginia. There are plenty of good books about the Mountain State, and the list gets longer all the time. Look for the likes of historian Otis Rice, novelists Denise Giardina and Mary Lee Settle, or the poet Louise McNeill. Or try anything by the late, great suspense writer, Davis Grubb — some night when you don't have to stay by yourself.

In short, we will be very pleased if our book leaves you wanting more.

I have spent more than a half-century learning about this state. For me, the process started in junior high school, where my classmates and I learned to recite the alphabetical list of counties: "Barbour, Berkeley, Boone, Braxton, Brooke, Cabell, Calhoun, Clay..."

I wish I could claim that I can still tick off all 55 of them. I can't. But even though I've long since forgotten that, the class nonetheless did its job — it instilled a curiosity about West Virginia that remains with me to this day.

Mixed in with curiosity is a considerable measure of

pride. Allow me to explain.

The first time I saw the State Capitol in Charleston I was a ten-year-old on a field trip. Its impressive hallways, ornate chambers and soaring dome left me in wide-eyed wonder. In the years since, my career as a newspaperman

MICHAEL KELLER

West Virginians are musical people, treasuring the tunes of their mountain heritage.

has made me a frequent visitor to the Capitol. Often, the rush of deadlines blinds me to its beauty. But, from time to time, I again find myself looking at the Capitol through the eyes of that ten-year-old boy. It's still beautiful, and I'm still proud that my state has such a handsome Capitol. And, yes, I'm proud, too, to be a West Virginian. I hope some of that shows in this book.

Huntington has been my lifelong home, and naturally the counties close to Huntington are the ones I know best.

A Marion County stream finds its way through Valley Falls State Park.

But over the years, it's been my good fortune to travel the length and breadth of the state, from Matewan to Martinsburg, Hamlin to Hillsboro, Wellsburg to White Sulphur Springs.

And as I've traveled I've discovered, as have many others, that there isn't just one West Virginia, there are many. West Virginia is incredibly diverse. It measures only 260 miles from east to west and just 237 miles from north to south. Yet, it reaches farther north than Pittsburgh, farther south than Richmond, almost as far east as Baltimore and farther west than Cleveland.

This diversity is what prompted our decision to arrange this book by regions, trying to offer a brief glimpse of each.

I say "our decision," because no project as ambitious as this one is the work of one individual. A great many people — far more than can be named here — have been involved in producing the book you now have in your hands.

First and foremost is our editor, Ken Sullivan, also editor of *Goldenseal*, West

The mists of summer cloak a barn near Wadestown.

Virginia's magazine of heritage and history. It was Ken who first asked me to undertake this book and then encouraged me at every step of the way. His reading and re-reading of the manuscript were invaluable. Without him, I doubt this book could have become a reality.

Photographer Gerald Ratliff not only produced dozens of fine original photographs for this volume but also spent many hours combing archives and tracking down the many other photos included here. He sought the best work of others to put beside his own, and it takes a confident, unselfish professional to do that. Gerry's efforts eventually brought more than a dozen fine photographers into the book, making it a showcase of our best photography.

Weaving our thousands of words and hundreds of pictures into a seamless tapestry was the challenge confronting book designer Anne H. Crozier. The "H" is for Huntington, and Anne, too, is a native West Virginian and proud of it. Proving more than equal to her task, she made us all look good and we appreciate it.

Countless other individuals contributed, many of them acknowledged in the credits section. Altogether they made *West Virginia: Mountain Majesty* a joint effort, genuine West Virginia teamwork. I am honored to have worked with them, and I am in their debt.

— James E. Casto

Right: At the Mountain State Art and Craft Fair.

WEST VIRGINIA STATE ARCHIVES

MICHAEL KELLER

Ohio River steamboats were popular subjects for postcard photographers of bygone days. This is the steamer "Royal," near Wheeling.

Opposite page - World-famous Fiesta ware is the product of Homer Laughlin China Company, a Northern Panhandle industrial giant. Fiesta, introduced in the Great Depression, is avidly collected today.

Northern Panhandle

CHAPTER 1

Formed at Pittsburgh where the Allegheny and the Monongahela rivers merge, the Ohio River first flows northwest, then abruptly reverses its course and heads southwest. A few miles later, it widens and separates, forming a large island in its middle. Rolling hills line the river's Ohio bank but on its eastern shore there is a small patch of flat land between the river and the hills. There the city of Wheeling grew up. In the nation's earliest years, Wheeling played an important role as a transportation gateway and an industrial center. And it was in Wheeling, amid the tumult of the Civil War, that the

new state of West Virginia was born on June 20, 1863.

But that's getting ahead of our story. Way ahead, for the history of West Virginia did not begin in 1863.

Archaeologists have determined that aboriginal man lived, or at least hunted, in West Virginia for thousands of years before the arrival of the first Europeans. Around 14,000 years ago, prehistoric hunters entered the Ohio and Kanawha valleys in pursuit of mastodons and other large animals, now extinct. Later peoples discovered permanent sources of food, pulling fish and shellfish from the rivers and harvesting wild fruits, nuts and berries.

Members of the Adena culture, which dates from roughly 500 B.C., left behind mysterious earthen and stone burial mounds throughout the Ohio Valley, none more impressive than the Grave Creek Mound at Moundsville, on the Ohio just downstream from Wheeling. It stands 61 feet high and contains an estimated 60,000 tons of earth. Joseph Tomlinson, first owner of the land where the mound is located, refused all proposals to open it. In 1838, a descendant, Jesse Tomlinson, believing that it might hold treasure, had it excavated. Workers found skeletons, pottery, some copper bracelets and a small sandstone tablet with

mysterious markings which have never been deciphered — or authenticated. Many believe the tablet a hoax. The Delf Norona Museum, opened beside the big mound in 1976, contains a permanent collection of Adena artifacts.

A legend has it that Wheeling, today the Northern Panhandle's largest city, took its name from the gruesome equivalent of a "No Trespassing" sign. Before the coming of the first white settlers, West Virginia provided a hunting grounds — and sometimes a battlefield — for the Iroquois, the Shawnee and other Native Americans, who saw the new arrivals as unwelcome intruders. Bloody encounters

The Northern Panhandle treasures its historic past through statuary, re-enactments and restorations. The Madonna of the Trail (left) commemorates pioneer motherhood. Civil War buffs (middle) stand guard in Hancock County, while Wellsburg's old Drovers Inn (below) still awaits guests.

were frequent. It is said one early trapper was beheaded by a Delaware warrior, and his head affixed to a pole as a warning to others. "Wheeling" roughly translates to "place of the head" in the Delaware tongue.

In 1749, an expedition under Pierre Joseph de Celoron de Beinville arrived at Wheeling Creek from French Canada and claimed the territory for Louis XV, but the hardy Scotch-Irish and German settlers who were the next arrivals ignored the French claim. They settled on the river flatland, and Wheeling was born.

In 1769, Ebenezer Zane and his two brothers fashioned a town from the scattered cabins of

MICHAEL KELLER

RICK LEE

The Mountain State was born at West Virginia Independence Hall in Wheeling (left), the former U.S. Custom House. Statehood was debated in the courtroom (above), now restored to its Civil War-era appearance.

Paying Homage to West Virginia Glass

West Virginia long has been famous for its glass. Once the state was home to as many as 500 glass plants, most of them small operations using methods little different from those devised by glassmakers in the Middle Ages. Today — as a result of changing tastes, foreign competition and the introduction of new technology — only a handful of those plants survive.

The Wheeling area was one of several locales in the state where the glass industry prospered. What it had in common with other areas of the state where glassmaking took hold was an abundant supply of natural gas, needed to fuel the intensely hot furnaces used to transform sand into glass, a river that provided a cheap and reliable means of transporting the finished product to market, and a skilled labor force.

STEPHEN J. SHALUTA, JR.

Glassmaking at the Brooke Glass Company in Wellsburg.

Carriage House Glass at Oglebay Park in Wheeling, which opened in 1993, pays homage to West Virginia's glass industry with a handsome museum housing an extensive collection of flint glass, lead crystal and cut glass produced by Wheeling-area companies from the early 1800s to the 1930s. The $1.8 million complex also includes a gift shop offering first-quality, handmade creations from West Virginia glass companies and artisans, and a demonstration center where visitors are able to see firsthand how delicate handblown glassware is made.

the original settlement. They brought their families, cleared land and planted farms. Life was hard, and Indian attacks frequent. In 1774, a wooden structure was built for the settlers' protection and later named Fort Henry when Patrick Henry was proclaimed the first rebel governor of Virginia. There, in a 1782 attack by Indians, Betty Zane won her legendary place in West Virginia history. As the story goes, the fort's defenders ran short of gunpowder and the nearest supply was in a cabin 150 yards away. "Tis better a young maid go," said Betty Zane, and braved the trip, carrying back the powder in her apron. The fort

was saved.

Probably the fiercest Indian fighter in West Virginia history was Lewis Wetzel. Brutally effective within the context of his time, Wetzel was a frontier hero. Today, his bloody exploits are regarded with mixed feelings. When he was 14, a band of Indians raided the family cabin near Wheeling, scalped his parents and kidnapped Lewis and his brother. Escaping some weeks later, young Wetzel vowed eternal vengeance.

A tale often told about Wetzel — maybe true, maybe not — is the story of the wild turkey. On several occasions, hunters were lured from the fort at Wheeling by the piercing call of

CITY HALL, WHEELING, W. VA.

Wheeling built a grand capitol to lure the state government back from Charleston in 1875. The building, which no longer stands, later served local government.

a wild turkey. But they never returned. Finally, Wetzel decided to try his luck. Slipping around behind where the turkey call originated, he saw an Indian's head emerge from the mouth of a cave. When the trickster cupped his hands to make his next turkey call, Wetzel shot him dead.

After the American Revolution, with the Indians subdued, Wheeling prospered as a gateway to the west — first via the busy Ohio River, then by the National Road and, finally, over the tracks of the Baltimore & Ohio Railroad.

West Virginians will tell you that the nation's first steamboat was launched by James Rumsey and demonstrated on the Potomac River at Shepherdstown in 1787. But it fell to Robert Fulton to make the steamboat a practical means of transportation. When Fulton's first steamboat on the Ohio, the *New Orleans*, stopped in Wheeling on its maiden voyage in 1811, a huge crowd paid 25 cents each to board and inspect the curious craft. Nobody had seen anything like it before. By 1830, Wheeling boatyards had built 19 steamboats and, as an

iron-making center, the city had supplied engines and boilers for many others built elsewhere. By the 1850s, three million passengers traveled the Ohio each year, and Wheeling was one of the river's busiest ports.

In 1806, President Thomas Jefferson pushed a bill through Congress authorizing construction of the National Road westward from Cumberland, Maryland. A mammoth undertaking, the road was 66 feet wide and cost a staggering $6,000 a mile. Work finally got underway in 1810, but only 10 miles were built the first year. The pace

quickened after that, and the road reached Wheeling and the banks of the Ohio in 1818.

Prior to construction of navigation locks on the Ohio, the river sometimes dried up to where travelers could cross the riverbed on foot. In high water, they had to cross by ferry. In 1849, the famed Wheeling Suspension Bridge was completed. More than 1,000 feet long, it was the first bridge to span the Ohio and at the time of its construction was the longest suspension bridge in the world. Designed by Charles Ellet Jr., the bridge was the object of a suit

The B&O station, now a community college, is among the city's 20th-century landmarks.

The Wheeling Suspension Bridge has carried traffic to Wheeling Island since 1849. The Island's river beaches were once favored by swimmers, such as the group (below) photographed at Belle Isle Beach.

filed by the state of Pennsylvania, which claimed it illegally obstructed the steamboat trade because the boats' stacks could not clear its deck during periods of high water. The U.S. Supreme Court ordered the bridge torn down, but Congress came to its rescue by declaring it a lawful structure. Less than two years later, Mother Nature did what the court couldn't when a wind storm blew the bridge down. Ellet rebuilt the bridge in an astonishing 40 days. Remodeled and strengthened several times over the years — most recently in the 1980s — the old bridge still is in use today.

The Baltimore & Ohio Railroad was completed to Wheeling in 1852 and the first B&O train arrived in the city on January 12, 1853, carrying more than 400 guests, including the governors of Maryland and Virginia. An elaborate 21-course banquet that night included lobster salad, capon with mushrooms and buffalo tongues. In 1908, the B&O built a $350,000 passenger station on Wheeling's Market Street, and for more than 50 years it hummed with the daily hustle and bustle of trains and travelers. That era ended in 1961 when the last passenger train left Wheeling. In 1975, the handsome old Beaux Arts building was purchased and remodeled to house West Virginia Northern

STEPHEN J. SHALUTA, JR.

GERALD S. RATLIFF

STEPHEN J. SHALUTA, JR.

Wheeling was once a hub of industry, and still is. The steel industry, including Weirton Steel (above), arose from such early predecessors as the Peter Tarr Iron Furnace in Hancock County (left). Workers (above right) produce the colorful dishes of the Homer Laughlin China Company.

Community College.

In the 1850s, Virginia had two official ports of entry, Norfolk and Wheeling. On March 21, 1859, a new U.S. Custom House was dedicated in Wheeling. Few of those attending the ceremonies could have guessed at the historic role the Custom House soon would play.

When Fort Sumter was fired on in April of 1861, Virginia joined other southern states in seceding from the Union. This alliance with the Confederacy was opposed by many in Virginia's western counties, where discontent with the government in Richmond had been building for years. Many in the west felt they had little in

common with the aristocratic residents of tidewater Virginia, with its large tobacco plantations carefully tended by slaves. The rugged land in the west was ill-suited for such plantations and, as a result, "backwoods" farmers grew corn and other grains and raised cattle, hogs or sheep. Slaves were few in the west.

The westerners remained loyal to the Union, and they felt that Virginia should, too. In 1861, they created the Restored Government of Virginia at Wheeling, a unionist government which sent representatives to Washington and acted in Virginia's name throughout the Civil War. The Restored Government of Virginia used the

Tobacco Town

In the early 1800s, a rugged vehicle rolled over the National Road from Cumberland, Maryland, to Wheeling and, eventually, on to other points west. It was the Conestoga, a covered wagon, named after the Conestoga tribe

Cigar makers posed proudly with their wares in this early photo, and Wheeling is still known for its tobacco products. Mail Pouch barn signs remain prominent landmarks throughout the region.

of the Iroquois Indians, and made by German settlers in the Conestoga Valley of Pennsylvania.

With their canvas tops and six-horse teams, the Conestogas were the very lifeline of early America, lumbering across mountain and meadow with cargoes weighing up to five tons. But it was slow progress, traveling at the rate of three or four miles an hour, and the wagon drivers had plenty of time on their hands. One of the drivers' main pleasures was to smoke a long, thin cigar made especially for them by the cigar makers of Wheeling, and called Conestoga cigars. That was kind of a mouthful, so before long the waggoners shortened it down to "stogie."

When the railroad stretched its tracks westward, the Conestoga wagon passed into history. But the stogies are still around — and still made in Wheeling by M. Marsh & Son.

Motion picture trivia buffs may know that a Wheeling stogie played a key role in the pivotal scene in *Fools' Parade*, the Jimmy Stewart movie made from the late Davis Grubb's novel of the same name. Grubb, best known for his *Night of the Hunter*, was a

Moundsville native who set much of his work in the mythical town of "Glory, West Virginia," patterned after his hometown. In *Fools' Parade*, ex-con Stewart threatens to use his stogie to light a bundle of dynamite and blow up a bank operated by worse crooks than those up at the State Pen. Much of the 1971 movie was filmed in and around Moundsville, including scenes shot at the old penitentiary.

Another survivor from the days when the Wheeling area had 65 tobacco companies is Mail Pouch brand chewing tobacco. First manufactured in the 1890s by the Bloch Brothers Tobacco Company, Mail Pouch was advertised with the slogan "Treat Yourself to the Best." Around the turn of the century, some unknown soul hit on the notion of painting the slogan on barns. The idea caught on and ultimately the company had a half-dozen painters on the

road, busily painting barns by the hundreds — not just in West Virginia and other nearby states, but as far away as California. Mail Pouch tobacco is still manufactured and sold by what is now the Helme Tobacco Company. But the days of the familiar Mail Pouch barn seem numbered. The company's last painter, Harley Warrick, retired in 1993.

Custom House as its capitol and it was there that delegates voted to create the new state of West Virginia. After winning approval by voters in the counties involved, by Congress and by President Abraham Lincoln, West Virginia became the nation's 35th state in 1863.

Over the years, many alterations and additions were made to the Custom House. In 1912, it was sold to private interests and at various times housed offices, a bank and even a nightclub. But in 1964, the state acquired it. After years of restoration work, the building — an impressive example of the Italian Renaissance Revival architectural style — was opened

GERALD S. RATLIFF ▼

STEPHEN J. SHALUTA, JR.

The steed above is the work of Wellsburg horse carver John Garton, while real horses run for the money (above right) at Mountaineer Park in neighboring Hancock County.

as West Virginia Independence Hall, where visitors can step back in time and listen to the echoes of the impassioned statehood debate.

After the Civil War, competition from Pittsburgh, Cincinnati and other cities eroded Wheeling's prominence as a transportation hub. Nonetheless, Wheeling and the Northern Panhandle continued to grow as an industrial center, a role it still plays today. What made that growth possible was a remarkable abundance of natural resources. Plentiful bituminous coal made the city a vital part of the nation's fuel-hungry iron and steel industry. The manufacture of cut iron nails became such a

specialty that for years Wheeling was known as the "Nail Capital of the World." Deposits of silica, sandstone and clay enabled the manufacture of glass, pottery and bricks. The processing of tobacco into cigars and chewing tobacco also was an important early industry, and remains so today.

It's estimated that in 1900, Wheeling and the Northern Panhandle contained fully a third of all the manufacturing facilities found in West Virginia. Northern Panhandle industry played a key role in World War I and an even more important one in World War II, when no commodity was more in demand than steel. In the 1940s, the Ohio Valley Board of Trade

A young angler tries his luck at Tomlinson Run State Park (above), while dinosaurs cavort as part of the Festival of Lights at Oglebay Park. The Victorian interior (below right) of Oglebay Mansion shows an elegant side of Northern Panhandle life.

bragged that Wheeling-area industry ranged "from A to Z," from automobile parts to zinc refining.

Today, the Northern Panhandle has not been immune to the "rust belt" woes that have afflicted so much of the nation's industry and, yes, it has its share of empty, deserted plants. But these are outnumbered by those still humming away, still producing steel and a myriad of other products. One of the panhandle's best-known companies, Wheeling-Pittsburgh Steel Corporation, founded in 1920, is today the nation's ninth largest integrated steelmaker. It produces 2.4 million tons of raw steel a year, has annual sales of $1 billion

and a work force of 5,400.

In 1982, when National Steel threatened to shut down its giant plant at Weirton, employees there took matters into their own hands and proceeded to buy the plant in what — at $366 million — was then the largest employee stock ownership plan (ESOP) in the nation. Weirton's workers took sharp pay cuts to make the plant competitive and eventually some lost their jobs when declining sales forced cuts in production. Today's payroll of 6,200 workers is roughly half the company's peak work force. Even so, the steelmaker is the largest private employer in West Virginia and one that, thanks to an investment of more than

The grounds of the Stifel Fine Arts Center in Wheeling (above) tempt artists with bountiful flowers. Fans of the musical arts flock to WWVA's "Jamboree USA" for such top country acts as Patty Loveless (left). The Jamboree's 1947 cast crowds the stage at bottom.

$500 million, is pioneering important new high-tech advances.

In the 1890s and the early years of this century, the Northern Panhandle's busy industrial plants attracted large number of European immigrants, both craftsmen and unskilled laborers, making it perhaps the most ethnically diverse section of the state. The panhandle attracted Germans, Irish, Italians, Poles, and Greeks, many of whom established their own churches and fraternal societies. That rich ethnic heritage is celebrated with annual events such as Weirton's International Food and Arts Festival and Wheeling's Upper Ohio Valley Italian Festival.

The plants produced an active trade union movement and labor leaders such as Samuel Gompers, Eugene V. Debs and John L. Lewis were frequent visitors to the region. Walter Reuther (1907-1970), president of the United Automobile Workers and the Congress of Industrial Organizations, was born in Wheeling, the son of a trade-union and Socialist activist.

Nowadays the Northern Panhandle attracts another kind of visitor — tourists in record number.

Many come to enjoy Oglebay Park, once the splendid summer estate of Cleveland

A Village Rich in History

With a population of only 1,139, the Northern Panhandle village of Bethany may contain more history per square foot than any other community in West Virginia. Chartered in 1853 by the Virginia Legislature, the village was home to Alexander Campbell, one of the 19th century's foremost scholars, debaters, educators and religious leaders.

Born in Ireland in 1788, Campbell emigrated to the United States in 1808 and died at Bethany in 1866 at age 77. He was the founder of the Disciples of Christ religious denomination and of Bethany College. Established in 1840, the college traces its roots to the Buffalo Seminary, a boarding school Campbell opened in 1818.

Today, history-minded visitors can visit a number of painstakingly restored buildings, including the Campbell Mansion, where the religious leader and educator lived for more than a half century. The three-story home originally was built by Campbell's father-in-law, John Brown, in 1793, and was later remodeled and enlarged several times, eventually growing to 27 rooms.

The mansion's dining room could seat 35 people and, since Campbell loved to entertain, frequently was full. Over the years, he hosted a number of famous men — including John C. Calhoun, Henry Clay, Daniel Webster, Jefferson Davis and James A. Garfield. One room of the mansion was decorated with handmade wallpaper, imported from France and identical to that used by Andrew Jackson in the hall of his Hermitage in Nashville, Tennessee. Built-in bookcases boasted doors of glass which, along with that in the windows, reportedly was the first glass brought to the region. On the grounds is a small hexagon-shaped structure Campbell used as a study. It was there that he wrote many of his 59 books.

Old Main, with its 122-foot tower, is the focal point of the historic Bethany College campus. Its construction was started in 1858, interrupted by the Civil War, and finished in 1872. Today, the restored structure is photographed and studied by the many architects and historians who visit it every year.

Old Meeting House was the second meeting house of the Bethany Church of Christ. Constructed by Campbell in 1852, the simple one-room sanctuary remains almost intact and features many of its original furnishings — including large, pot bellied stoves, a small pulpit and oil lamp chandeliers.

Pendleton Heights is the official residence of Bethany College's presidents. It was constructed in 1841 by William Kimbrough Pendleton, the college's first vice president and professor of natural philosophy. Pendleton succeeded Campbell as president on the latter's death. A graduate of the University of Virginia and the son of one of the commonwealth's leading families, Pendleton married successively two of Campbell's daughters. He sold Pendleton Heights to the college in 1889.

The Bethany campus saw the founding of Delta Tau Delta and the national Greek fraternity's founding house, built between 1853 and 1856, has been preserved and restored.

Old Main is the centerpiece at Bethany College.

GERALD S. RATLIFF

industrialist Earl V. Oglebay, who died in 1926 and willed it to the city of Wheeling. Today, the 1,500-acre park offers golfing, skiing and horseback riding. Its Wilson Lodge, with 204 rooms, is a popular convention site. The Mansion Museum offers a glimpse of sophisticated living at the turn of the century. And the park's Good Zoo features 65 acres of North American animals in a natural habitat, designed especially to appeal to youngsters. The popular "Festival of Lights" sparkles throughout Oglebay and downtown Wheeling each year, from November through early February. Millions of holiday lights draw busload after busload of admirers in what

DAVID E. FATTALEH

WEST VIRGINIA STATE ARCHIVES

The Northern Panhandle is a surprisingly urban place for a rural state. Brick townhouses crowd the sidewalks in downtown Wheeling (above), while the photo of Wellsburg's Charles Street typifies smaller cities of an earlier day.

has become one of the region's most popular tourist attractions.

Music is the drawing card for visitors to the Capitol Music Hall, at 1015 Main Street. "Jamboree USA," broadcast live from the theater every Saturday night on radio station WWVA, is the nation's second oldest live country music program. It first aired in 1933. The old theater, which welcomed its first audience in 1928, also is home to the Wheeling Symphony. In summers, the symphony performs outdoors at Oglebay.

Another popular attraction for Wheeling visitors is the Center Market. There was a time, not so very long ago, when every city of any size had a market house, where local farmers and artisans could sell their produce and products. Most long since have vanished, victims of progress. But Wheeling has not one but two, which offer an array of shopping and dining opportunities. Built in 1853, the Upper Market House is the only cast-iron columned market house in the United States. The Lower Market House, built in 1890, is a Romanesque brick structure.

Wheeling has a number of fine old Victorian homes, built by the city's early industrialists

and business leaders, some of which are open for guided tours or available for bed and breakfast. Wheeling Island, the western end of the Suspension Bridge and more recently a stepping stone for Interstate 70, is a treasure trove of turn-of-the-century building styles.

A short drive north from Wheeling is the Drover's Inn, an authentic 1848 country inn with handcrafted furnishings. Venture further north, to the tip of the Northern Panhandle, and you'll find the Homer Laughlin China Company, the world's largest manufacturer of dinnerware. The company is famous for its Fiesta ware, a Depression-era collector's item recently brought back into

GEORGE J. KOSSUTH

GERALD S. RATLIFF

Grave Creek Mound overlooks the city of Moundsville and the old state penitentiary, as photographed (above right) by the eminent Wheeling photographer, George James Kossuth.

STEPHEN J. SHALUTA, JR.

Sunrise at Tomlinson Run Lake.

production by popular demand.

Travel south from Wheeling to Moundsville and you'll find — just across the street from the Grave Creek Mound — the old West Virginia State Penitentiary, now vacant since inmates were moved to the state's new Mount Olive correctional complex in Fayette County. The oldest part of the grim, fortress-like penitentiary dates back to the Civil War. With its inmates gone, the old prison has been transformed into a tourist attraction. Guided tours conducted by former guards give visitors a chance to see what daily life was like behind the prison's 30-foot-high walls. The tour includes a glimpse of "Old Sparky," the prison's electric chair.

Just outside of Moundsville is surely one of the strangest sights to be seen anywhere in West Virginia — the Palace of Gold. Built by devotees of the Hare Krishna faith, it has been called the "Taj Mahal of the West."

The Washington's Lands Museum of Ravenswood recalls earlier days in the Ohio Valley, as well as a name famous to the region.

Opposite Page - A lone oak stands sentry in Jackson County.

Mid-Ohio Valley

CHAPTER 2

In October of 1770, his services as commander of the Continental Army and first President of the United States still ahead of him, a 38-year-old George Washington traveled by canoe down the Ohio River, from what is now Pittsburgh to the site of present-day Point Pleasant. Washington, with a party of other Virginians and two Indians hired as guides, was intent on exploring the land along the river's south bank, where he hoped to establish a new colony.

That dream was not to be. Nonetheless, the thriving West Virginia communities that now dot the Mid-Ohio Valley are eloquent testimony to the bold

vision of Washington and people like him.

Washington's diary of his nine-week trip, faded but still readable, is now in the Library of Congress. In it he commented on the "remarkably crooked" condition of the Ohio, which was "choked up with Fallen Trees." He noted that he and his companions saw "innumerable quantities of Turkeys, and many Deer watering, and browsing on the Shore side, some of which we killd." And he complained that squatters already were "Marking all the Lands that are valuable."

As a result of this 1770 trip and subsequent surveys made in his behalf, Washington obtained patents for 34,000

acres in what is now West Virginia. Today, just south of Ravenswood at the Great Bend in the Ohio River, the Washington's Lands Museum displays a collection of artifacts that includes early land-grant documents signed by Patrick Henry. On the surrounding park grounds a log house exhibits period furnishings of the 1840s and the trappings of an old country store.

Washington, though disappointed in his own colonizing effort, remained a fervent advocate of western settlement. Perhaps because he had glimpsed the remarkable beauty of the Ohio Valley with his own eyes, he was one of the first Americans

to sense the importance of westward expansion.

And expand the new nation did. With the end of the American Revolution, a tide of settlers, many of them veterans of the war with the British, swarmed into the Ohio Valley. In the absence of good roads, the Ohio River served as a broad, watery highway leading west.

These new arrivals were a varied lot. Some were men of wealth looking for chances to invest their capital. Many were farmers. Others were blacksmiths, gunsmiths, harnessmakers or other artisans. Many a future merchant left his home in the East, traveled to Pittsburgh, bought a flatboat (or

DAVID E. FATTALEH

©VAN SLIDER

Tyler County farm scene, blanketed by snow.

History and pre-history abound throughout the valley. The monument at left commemorates the 1774 Battle of Point Pleasant, which pitted Virginia militia against Shawnee warriors. Archaeologists excavated Blennerhassett Island (lower left) while researching the island's past.

GERALD S. RATLIFF

a share in one) and then headed downstream with a load of goods.

These flatboats replaced the canoes of the Indians and the rafts of the earliest settlers. Before long the flatboats gave way to keelboats, propelled by men who stood on the deck and pushed the boat forward with long poles which they thrust into the riverbed. Unlike flatboats, the keelboats could travel upstream. In 1811, the first steamboat appeared on the Ohio. The *New Orleans* was a success, and by 1835 nearly 700 steamboats were traveling the Ohio.

On its maiden trip down the Ohio, the *New Orleans* stopped to refuel at Parkersburg, today the Mid-Ohio Valley's largest city. Parkersburg traces its origin to 1773, when Robert Thornton staked out a claim to lands extending in a northern direction from the confluence of the Ohio and Little Kanawha rivers. Ten years later, Captain Alexander Parker, a Pennsylvanian who served in the Revolution, purchased Thornton's claim, paying $50 for 1,400 acres. But Parker died without ever seeing his land. It fell to Captain James Neal, who had been sent to survey the tract, to build, in 1785, its first settlement — a cluster of log cabins around a blockhouse. By the late 1790s, the little community had grown and a town plan was drawn up by John Stockley who named it

America's petroleum industry was incubated in the western counties of West Virginia, using technology perfected in earlier salt-well drilling. Sistersville (above) was one of the oil boom towns while the Ritchie County derrick (far left) still stands as a reminder of earlier days.

Monongahela Power Company's coal-fired generating plant at Willow Island typifies the valley's major energy producers.

Newport. But that name didn't stick. In 1810, when the town was officially surveyed, it was re-named "Parkersburg" in honor of Captain Parker.

In the steamboat era, Parkersburg was a bustling place. The 1838 completion of the Northwestern Turnpike, connect-ing Winchester, Virginia, with Parkersburg (along the present-day route of U.S. 50) established the city as a thriving center of commerce. Nine years later, construction of the Staunton-Parkersburg Turnpike brought more business — and more people — to the busy river town.

But it was the coming of the railroad that triggered Parkersburg's greatest growth. A branch of the Baltimore & Ohio Railroad reached Parkersburg in 1857, but its trains initially had to be ferried across to Ohio by barges. The first stone for the B&O Railroad Bridge was laid on July 9, 1869, and the first train crossed on January 7, 1871. Still in use today, the 7,140-foot span was at the time of its opening the longest railroad bridge in the world. It cost $1 million to build, and legend has it that the B&O borrowed the money from financier Hetty Green, the eccentric and colorful "Witch of Wall Street."

In 1860, the first oil wells were drilled at Burning Springs, about 40 miles up the Little Kanawha River from Parkers-

The Smoot recalls pleasant memories for generations of Parkersburgers.

Parkersburg is the metropolis of the Mid-Ohio Valley. The postcard view looks down Third Street toward the Wood County Courthouse, while the photo (left) shows the impressive building as it appears today.

burg. Soon the Wirt County village was producing what seemed like an ocean of oil, and unfortunately had become an alluring target for Confederate raiders. After the Civil War, new deep-drilling techniques produced a second oil boom in the area. Wells also yielded natural gas, originally considered a nuisance byproduct of petroleum.

Today, Parkersburg remains a center of industry. A dozen nationally known chemical companies operate plants in the area. The largest two, DuPont and GE Plastics, are located adjacent to each other along the Ohio, eight miles south of the

manufacturing system, produces bulk plastics for the automobile, appliance and tool industries. GE Plastics is the world's largest manufacturer of ABS engineering thermoplastics.

Another major local employer is the Ames Company, which claims to be the oldest continuously operating manufacturer in the United States. The company traces its roots to Captain John Ames, a Massachusetts blacksmith who dared defy the British ban against making steel shovels in the American Colonies. Over the years, the company thrived by continuing

The Mountain State Art and Craft Fair

West Virginians always have been proud of their handy ways, and nowhere is that pride more evident than at the Mountain State Art and Craft Fair, held each summer at Cedar Lakes, near Ripley.

Established in 1963 as part of the state's Centennial celebration, the fair is now a genuine extravaganza. Each year, jurors have the difficult task of picking artists and craftspeople to participate in the multi-day event.

Stroll down an aisle at the fair and you'll see booths featuring wooden candlesticks turned on a foot-powered lathe, decorated glass, red and white woven aprons, oak baskets, spun pewter, folk toys, quilts, pottery and more. Turn down another row and there's even more to discover. Plus, there's plenty of old-time mountain music, craft demonstrations, storytelling and folk dancing to enjoy.

Ah, and then there's the food. Non-profit groups prepare hearty country cuisine for hungry fair-goers — buckwheat cakes and sausage, cornbread and beans, home-made ice cream. Fifteen thousand ears of roasted corn are sold each year at the fair, along with 4,000 country ham sandwiches and dinners (that's a ton of ham), some 7,000 barbecued chicken dinners and, of course, countless hot dogs, hamburgers and soft drinks.

Given the variety of the work that's on display, there's no such thing as a "typical" artisan at the Mountain State Art and Craft Fair. But, as a representative example, consider master woodcarver Herman Hayes of Hurricane, who for many years was a fixture at the Jackson County event.

A retired Methodist minister, Hayes has been many things in his varied life. He's a former middleweight boxer and one-time vacuum cleaner salesman. But first, last and always he's been a woodcarver, turning out whimsical pieces such as his "Tower of Babel," which includes 150 little carved people carrying bricks to the top of the tower.

Hayes says his method is simple: Start carving and see what happens. "Most of my carpentry I develop into what I end up with," he says. "That way it makes no difference if I make a mistake."

He works in a little shop off his living room, supplementing his knife with a mallet and chisel when he works on larger pieces. "When I get fired up, wanting to get something finished, I stay up till midnight," he says, with a twinkle in his eye.

Corn on the cob brings smiling eyes to a young fair-goer at Cedar Lakes. Herman Hayes (below) was a resident craftsman for many years.

GERALD S. RATLIFF

shovels, as have our troops in every conflict since, including the Persian Gulf War. Ames came to Parkersburg in the 1930s, when it bought a plant built by Baldwin Tool Works in the early 1900s. Today, Ames offers a wide line of hand tools, virtually all of them made in two sprawling Parkersburg plants.

Parkersburg residents, like many West Virginians, have a strong sense of history and are working hard to preserve their heritage. The city includes some of the finest examples of Victorian architecture found anywhere in the state. Many of the structures, which date from 1850 to 1910, are private homes and not open to the public. But others welcome visitors. The Cook House was built in 1829 by

The Blennerhassett Hotel was built by William N. Chancellor, whose former home (below left) is another of Parkersburg's landmarks.

Tillinghast Cook, a son of Joseph Cook, one of the area's first settlers. Bricks for this small Federal-style house were fired on the site and the wood was cut nearby. Sandstone used to build the Wood County Courthouse, begun in 1899, was quarried not far away, at Quincey Hill. The Blennerhassett Hotel is a chateau-like, Queen Anne Style structure built by William N. Chancellor. Closed for several years, it was given an eloquent renovation in 1986 and today again welcomes weary travelers.

Another Parkersburg

1930 and for more than a half century was a mecca for local film fans. The Smoot closed its doors in 1986 and was facing the wrecking ball when, at the last minute, it was rescued by concerned citizens. Its burgundy and cream color decor was restored, along with its fancy gilt molding. Many of the old theater's original features remain intact: Trap doors in the stage floor (which was made of maple and pine to vary the dancers' tapping sounds), a 65-foot stage height to accommodate the largest scenery, and gas burners

Fresh-water sailors find pleasure on the Ohio (above left) but for generations the preferred form of travel were grand sternwheel steamers such as the one above.

The Ohio Valley today is characterized by the beauty of nature and the works of human builders, such as this river scene near Paden City (center) and the bridges of Parkersburg.

Museum, housed in a vintage building on Third Street, features an impressive collection of tools and equipment, along with photographs recalling the city's days as a boom town.

Among the Mid-Ohio Valley's premiere historical attractions is Blennerhassett Island, located in the Ohio River two miles downstream from Parkersburg. Small sternwheelers ferry visitors to the island, where they're welcomed by costumed docents who tell the bittersweet story of exiled Irish aristocrat Harman Blennerhassett and his young wife.

Born in County Kerry in 1764, Harman scandalized his family and friends by marrying his beautiful young niece, Margaret. The couple fled to America, eventually making their way down the Ohio River. In 1798, they landed on the nameless patch of land that would become known as Blennerhassett Island. There they lived in an abandoned log blockhouse for three years, while they supervised the building of a magnificent mansion in the wilderness. Constructed in the shape of a horseshoe and lavishly furnished, the big house was a showplace where the Blennerhassetts regularly entertained travelers who made their way down the river.

One such guest, who arrived in 1806, was Aaron Burr.

Margaret and Harman Blennerhassett built a dream on their Ohio River island, now represented by the reconstructed mansion (above). The Native American crafts village reminds us of earlier occupants of Blennerhassett Island.

Two years earlier, Burr — then Vice President of the United States — had killed Alexander Hamilton in a duel. With warrants out for his arrest, a bitter Burr was plotting an invasion of Mexico with the idea of setting himself up as its ruler. Searching for financial bankers, he heard of Harman and visited the island to seek his support. Harman eagerly threw in his lot.

When word of the plot reached President Thomas Jefferson, he ordered both men arrested. A unit of the Virginia militia arrived at the island to arrest Harman but found he had set off down the Ohio to join Burr. The soldiers briefly detained Margaret but then let her go. She quickly loaded what items she could on a flatboat and followed her husband down the river. Although Harman (like Burr) eventually was acquitted of treason, the Blennerhassetts never saw their Ohio River island again. In 1811, a fire destroyed the wooden mansion. But today it has been reconstructed on its original foundation and, furnished with period antiques, revives the splendor of years gone by.

Another popular Mid-Ohio Valley attraction is the Fenton Art Glass Company, located in Williamstown, just north of Parkersburg. Fenton is world famous for its handmade glass and every year thousands of

©VAN SLIDER

The valley and its river, near New Martinsville.

Taming the Stubborn Ohio

The Ohio River down which the valley's first settlers traveled was an unpredictable stream. In summer, the river often dried to the size of a creek and in many places was shallow enough to wade across. At other times of the year, it would become a raging torrent that quickly overflowed its banks. George Washington was among the first of many travelers to complain about its stubborn, difficult nature.

GERALD S. RATLIFF

Robert C. Byrd Locks and Dam.

The Ohio River was tamed — and made suitable for year-round navigation — by a series of dams constructed by the U.S. Army Corps of Engineers. The first was constructed in 1885, at Davis Island, just downstream from Pittsburgh, but it would be 1929 before the river-long system was completed. And by then there already was an obvious need to modernize it.

In 1938, the first of a new generation of Ohio River dams, the Gallipolis Locks and Dam, just downstream from Point Pleasant, was dedicated, but the onset of World War II prevented the construction of any others.

During the war, river traffic grew dramatically and, once the fighting was over and the nation returned to a peacetime footing, the river's modernization resumed. In the intervening years, the steam-powered paddlewheelers had given way to powerful diesel-powered towboats capable of pushing mammoth barges, lashed together in multi-barge "tows" far larger than veteran rivermen had dared dream of. To handle these large tows, new dams built on the Ohio included 1,200-foot locks.

Soon, only the Gallipolis Dam was left with the older, 600-foot lock that had once

been the river standard. This meant that most tows using it had to be broken into two sections and locked through separately, a time-consuming process. And on the river, time is money.

After years of study, the Corps of Engineers decided to construct a new canal that would bypass the old locks and dam and, in the process, shave hours off the time that each barge tow would require to make its way past Gallipolis.

The canal — a mammoth undertaking that required the excavation of 14 million cubic yards of earth and the pouring of 800,000 yards of concrete — cost $224 million to build. But rivermen say that over the years it will more than pay for itself by speeding the flow of cargo.

The new canal, dedicated October 10, 1992, was built on the West Virginia side of the river. And, fittingly enough, Congress only days before voted to change the name of the Gallipolis facility to the Robert C. Byrd Locks and Dam, recognizing the veteran West Virginia lawmaker's years of championing the project.

people tour the factory to watch its master craftsmen at work. The company was founded by Frank Leslie Fenton in 1905 at Martin's Ferry, Ohio, as a glass decorating operation. In the fall of the same year, he decided to build another plant in Williamstown. This new facility was involved in the complete manufacture of glass items, from raw materials to finished product. Three brothers — John, Charles and James — joined the firm and eventually another brother, Robert, also got involved. Only John decided to move on, leaving three Fentons to operate what would become one of the state's best known glass factories.

Memories rest quietly at a Jackson County churchyard.

TODD A. HANSON

Wood County's Henderson Hall is more than a century and a half old.

▲ DAVID E. FATTALEH ▼

Proud work of Fenton Glass.

Today, Fenton makes everything from art glass items prized by collectors to spit sinks used in dentists' offices. "We don't just make decorative baskets and vases," says Bill Fenton, chairman of the board and one of a dozen family members still involved in the company. "You have to diversify. You can't put it all into one thing."

Fenton prides himself on his company's ability to keep pace with the times, as evidenced by his regular appearances on cable television's QVC Network, vigorously pitching Fenton glassware to home-shopping viewers.

Nearby, in the small town of Boaz, stands Henderson Hall. George Washington Henderson began his home in 1836, building the main part between 1856 and 1859. The massive three-story Italianate mansion includes its original furnishings and several generations of memorabilia.

The oil and gas boom that hit Parkersburg also was felt upriver, in the little town of Sistersville, where the historic Wells Inn opened its doors on January 15, 1895. It immediately became a popular stopover for those in the oil and gas industry, as well as other business travelers. The historic hotel fell on hard times in the 1980s, however, as fewer and

Islands in the Stream

Naturalists at work at the new Ohio River Islands Wildlife Refuge.

fewer people passed through town. Eventually, its owners closed the doors and put the old place up for auction. Today the hotel is open again with new ownership, new management and a new lease on life. And it's in the midst of a $1 million renovation aimed at returning its former splendor.

Located approximately 25 miles east of Parkersburg is North Bend State Park and the 60-mile North Bend Rail Trail, part of a growing network of West Virginia trails fashioned from abandoned railroad rights-of-way. Originally the B&O's main line and an engineering marvel in its day, it's part of the 5,500-mile coast-to-coast

As recently as the 1890s, the Ohio River contained hundreds of islands, but over the years many were lost to commercial dredging and navigation projects. Those that remain provide nesting spots for blue herons and other waterfowl and are home to beaver, mink, muskrat and deer.

To protect those animal residents, more than two dozen islands — totalling 3,500 acres — have been designated by the federal government as the Ohio River Islands National Wildlife Refuge. Creation of the refuge was a joint public-private effort, involving the U.S. Fish and Wildlife Service, the Nature Conservancy, Ducks Unlimited and a number of private companies.

Rich in biological significance, the islands represent a mosaic of bottomland hardwoods, wetlands and various life forms both common and rare to the area. They also serve migratory birds such as the black duck and the king rail, as well as the endangered pink musket mussel.

The prime mover in obtaining federal approval — and funding — for the Ohio River Islands Refuge was U.S. Senator Robert C. Byrd. At 1992 ceremonies officially dedicating the

refuge, Byrd noted that its islands once "were considered obstacles, nothing more than mounds in the river. But these islands supported many other life forms before man arrived here. By setting them aside now, birds, animals, fish and other water creatures will be able to flourish and use those islands much as their ancestors did thousands of years ago."

The refuge extends along the Ohio for 362 miles. The islands within its boundaries are located in Pennsylvania, West Virginia and Kentucky. But most are in the West Virginia stretch of the river, making this the first national wildlife refuge in the Mountain State.

Over the years, the islands have been used for a variety of purposes. Many show evidence of past Indian encampments, farming, logging, recreational camping, commercial dredging, mooring, construction and oil drilling. One of the largest, Buffington Island, was the scene of a brief but bloody Civil War battle.

The Fish and Wildlife Service is buying the islands one by one, as funds become available and negotiations can be concluded with their private owners. Islands are being added only by purchase from willing sellers, not by condemnation. Money for buying the islands comes from the federal Land and Water Conservation Fund, which benefits from the tax revenues paid by operators of offshore oil rigs.

Boaters are welcome to stop and visit the islands during the day. But no overnight mooring or camping is allowed.

The postcard (above) offers an overview of the Tyler County town of Sistersville. The ornate interior of Henderson Hall (left) represents the valley's 19th century heyday.

American Discovery Trail.

Venture down the Ohio River from Parkersburg and you come to Point Pleasant, built where the Kanawha River joins the Ohio. This was where, in 1770, George Washington and his fellow travelers camped, then turned and made their way back up the river. People in Point Pleasant like to boast that Tu-Endie-Wei — the "point between two waters," as the Indians called it — was the scene of the first battle of the American Revolution.

Historians point out that the Battle of Point Pleasant was actually part of Lord Dunmore's War, one of a series of Indian conflicts. The October 10, 1774, battle between the Virginia militia, led by General Andrew Lewis, and the Mingo and Shawnee warriors, under Chief Cornstalk, broke the power of the Indians in the Ohio Valley.

Today, the site is a small park, with an 84-foot granite shaft that commemorates the battle. The park also includes what's said to be the oldest surviving log home in the Kanawha Valley. Built in 1796 by Walter Newman, it housed a tavern — and Newman's family of 13 children.

Near Point Pleasant, the West Virginia State Farm Museum — 31 buildings on 50 acres of land — offers a glimpse of yesteryear's farm life through exhibits of antique farm tools and equipment.

But farming is by no means a vanished way of life in the Mid-Ohio Valley. The valley still is home to hundreds of small farms, many of them owned and

Ohio Valley farms and farmers share the countryside with wild inhabitants of the region. The man at right tries a vintage tractor at the West Virginia State Farm Museum.

operated by industrial workers who have full-time jobs in Parkersburg or Point Pleasant and do their farm chores before or after their "day job." Fertile bottomland along the Ohio River is devoted to dairy herds or planted with corn, hay and other crops. A few miles back in the hills are beef cattle operations and sheep flocks. Bacon, ham, lamb, honey, milk, small fruits and vegetables — all are produced in the valley. Dairy farms ship milk to larger metropolitan centers. Each year tons of cabbage, beans, tomatoes, sweet corn and potatoes are shipped to markets as far away as Dayton, Cleveland, and Pittsburgh.

The Mid-Ohio Valley's many part-time farmers have their roots in the soil and lend the region a welcome stability that's rare in today's fast-paced, rapidly changing America.

Excitement packs the stadium at West Virginia University on Saturday afternoons throughout the fall.

Opposite Page - Hot air balloons rise at Morgantown's Mountaineer Balloon Festival.

Mountaineer Country

CHAPTER 3

California has the San Andreas Fault. West Virginia has Mountaineer Stadium. Tremors traced to the fault regularly jolt Californians. They're called earthquakes. Similar shocks can be felt on certain fall Saturdays in West Virginia. Their epicenter? The stadium in Morgantown, jammed with a blue-and-gold sea of 70,000 frenzied fans. It's called football, West Virginia University style.

But West Virginia University is more than football. Much more. For more than 125 years it's been one of the state's greatest assets. And today WVU is the northern anchor of a rapidly growing corridor that extends south along Interstate

79 to the Clarksburg-Bridgeport area. Increasingly, the I-79 corridor is attracting high-technology jobs unheard of just a few short years ago. And, in many instances, what's making those jobs possible is the availability of WVU's expertise.

The university's 14 schools and colleges offer 23,000 full-time students — from all 55 West Virginia counties, almost every U.S. state and a long list of foreign countries — a choice of 175 bachelor's, master's, doctoral and professional degree programs, ranging from aerospace engineering to wood industries. And 24 WVU students have been chosen to receive prized Rhodes Scholarships to study at Oxford University.

In the beginning — February 7, 1867 — the school had six professors and six students. West Virginia had joined the land-grant educational movement that was to transform America. The Morrill Act, signed by President Abraham Lincoln on July 2, 1862, offered 30,000 acres of federal land for each congressman in every state that agreed to sell the land and use the proceeds to establish a college that would teach agriculture and mechanical arts. The new institution first was known as the Agriculture College of West Virginia, but in 1868 the name was changed to West Virginia University.

In those early years, WVU students were awakened each

morning by the firing of a cannon at 6 a.m. and had to retire to their rooms each evening when the curfew bell rang at 9 p.m. They were forbidden to swear, drink, smoke, play billiards or watch theatrical performances.

That ban on theater must have been short-lived, for when the first WVU football team took the field in 1891 it was partially financed with proceeds from a student production of Shakespeare's *Richard III*. The all-male cast included many of the football players. The play's director, Melville Davisson Post, later became a popular mystery writer.

Today, WVU consists of 158 buildings on 673 acres, split

WVU is an institution with an historic past and exciting future. Woodburn Hall (left) is the centerpiece of the historic downtown campus, while the modernistic PRT (below left) carries students toward the Evansdale campus. Ruby Memorial Hospital (below) offers high tech medical and research facilities.

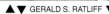 ▲▼ GERALD S. RATLIFF ▼

between two campuses, the Downtown Campus and the Evansdale-Health Sciences Campus, where Ruby Memorial Hospital offers state-of-the-art facilities for clinical and research medicine. One of the latest innovations: Mountaineer Doctor Television — or MDTV, for short — which links Morgantown with a dozen rural clinics around the state. A two-way audio and video system, MDTV allows live interchanges between rural doctors and their patients and the medical specialists in Morgantown. Patients and doctors at each end of the system can hear, see and speak with one another. And MDTV also enables the immediate, crystal-clear transmission of X-rays, CAT scans, laboratory slides and other diagnostic materials.

The university's two campuses are a handsome mix of modern structures and traditional buildings, including the historic buildings that make up Woodburn Circle, the oldest part of the campus.

On a warm, sunny, fall day, the university bustles with activity. Students gather on the Mountainlair plaza while others take long walks, perhaps window shopping on High Street in downtown Morgantown. Once winter arrives and the snow begins to blanket Morgantown, the campus sparkles, and Woodburn Hall, aglow with

Jerry West

As a basketball player at East Bank High School in the 1950s, Jerry West set records in field goals scored, free throws made and total points. And he's been setting records ever since — as a stand-out player at West Virginia University and an all-time great for the National Basketball Association's Los Angeles Lakers.

Jerry West was born May 28, 1938, near Cheylan, just outside Charleston. The family's mailing address was "Cabin Creek, West Virginia" and eventually the future basketball star would find himself tagged as "Zeke from Cabin Creek."

West remembers what it was like to dribble a ball on the hard-packed West Virginia dirt. The young boy dribbled, shot — and dreamed.

"I was my own best friend," he says of those days. "I was everything, actually. Player, coach, announcer, even the time-keeper. It was amazing to me how many times in those imaginary games there'd be one second left, my team one point down and me with the ball, and I'd miss and — the really amazing part — there would still be time for another shot, or 10."

Not too many years later, West would make a 60-foot shot at the buzzer to send a 1970 NBA championship game into overtime. It *was* amazing.

It's a long way from Cabin Creek to the NBA. West credits his high school coach, Roy Williams, with helping him take the first steps along the way — instilling in the young player a stubborn determination to learn all aspects of the game — shooting, defense, passing and play-making. In his senior year at East Bank, West averaged 34.2 points per game and became the first player in West Virginia to score more than 900 points in a single season.

WVU basketball coach Fred Schaus (who later would go on to be general manager of the Lakers) recruited West. As a sophomore, West played on the Mountaineer team that was ranked number one in the country in 1958.

During his three-year varsity career at WVU, West averaged 24.8 points and 13.3 rebounds per game, while shooting 50.6 percent. He was voted Most Valuable Player each of his three years on varsity. He played on the Pan-American Games team in 1958, was voted Most Valuable Player in the NCAA "Final Four" in 1959, and was a member of the U.S. team that won a gold medal at the 1960 Olympics in Rome.

The Lakers, just then picking up to move from Minneapolis to Los Angeles, drafted West in the first round in 1960. His first season as a professional was disappointing but he rebounded the next year, pushing his scoring from 17.6 points per game to 30.8. One of the highlights of that second season: a 63-point effort against the New York Knickerbockers, a single-game scoring record for guards.

By this time, nobody was calling him "Zeke" any more. His new nickname: "Mr. Clutch," a recognition of his amazing ability to win in highly pressured situations.

West had a distinguished 14-year career in the NBA and still holds many of the Lakers team records. He was hired as general manager of the Lakers in 1982 and proceeded to build the team into a sports dynasty. He was appointed Lakers president in 1988.

The fame and recognition haven't changed Jerry West. Long-time friends says he has remained what he was the day he first showed up on the WVU campus — "modest, respectful and courteous."

Visitors to his home will see few reminders of his legendary career: His gold medal from the 1960 Olympics, a painting of him done by a former teammate and the ball with which he scored his 25,000th point. The ball, he notes, has scored a few more in his driveway, where some of his five sons have used it in pickup games.

West Virginians recall Jerry West as high school and college stand-out.

WEST VIRGINIA STATE ARCHIVES

Monongalia County history, rural and urban. The Forks of Cheat Baptist Church (above) traces its roots back to colonial days. Streetcars once clattered through Morgantown (left).

Preston County's Big Sandy Creek is one of many West Virginia streams to offer whitewater adventure.

hundreds of white lights, brightens the night. Springtime brings new life to the campus as the flowers and trees bloom, and students' thoughts turn to spring break and summer vacation.

A familiar part of daily life at WVU is the Personal Rapid Transit system, which shuttles students quickly between the university's campuses and downtown Morgantown. Built by the U.S. Department of Transportation as a demonstration project, the PRT consists of driverless, computer-directed, electric-powered cars that travel an elevated concrete and steel guideway. Students are issued a PRT card when they enroll and ride the system without further

charges.

Futuristic innovations such as MDTV and the PRT offer a marked contrast to historic Morgantown, chartered in 1785 and named for the Morgan family, among the earliest white settlers in western Virginia. Symbolic of Morgantown's proud past is the Old Stone House, built in 1784 from native sandstone. Over the years, the two-story house has been a tavern, tannery, church and home. Today, it's a craft shop. Another intriguing glimpse of yesteryear can be seen at the Seneca Glass Factory, which once produced fine crystal stemware but today houses retail shops. Glassmaking once was a thriving

©VAN SLIDER

The road above leads to a Barbour County farmstead, while Valley Falls State Park (right) represents a wilder terrain.

GERALD S. RATLIFF

to replace its obsolete fingerprint identification system with new "state-of-the-art" technology, the Bureau opted to move outside Washington.

"Why not West Virginia?" asked Senator Robert C. Byrd. Why not, indeed. Byrd was instrumental in convincing the FBI to move to the Mountain State, where it found a more cost-efficient environment. Site preparation got underway in 1991 and construction the following year.

The centerpiece of the multi-building complex is the stunning Main Building, which consists of five three-story office towers. It includes a 500-seat auditorium, a 600-seat cafeteria, a fitness exercise area and

employee lounges on each floor of each module. At present, the complex employs about 1,200 people. Eventually, the workforce is expected to number 2,500. About 250 people transferred from the Washington area, the remainder hired locally.

The influx of FBI jobs has prompted new home construction throughout Mountaineer Country. FBI employees live in Morgantown, Fairmont and Grafton and as far south as Weston and Buckhannon. And the economic "spin-off" from the FBI complex is creating even more new jobs.

STEPHEN J. SHALUTA, JR. ▲

The Sutton Lake dam impounds the waters of Elk River.

Opposite Page - Bass fisherman try their luck at Stonewall Jackson Lake, West Virginia's newest.

West Virginia Heartland

CHAPTER 4

Traditionally, the U.S. Army Corps of Engineers names its new dams after the nearest community with a post office. But when the Corps undertook construction of a new flood-control project in Nicholas County, the nearest town was Gad. Officials only briefly considered the name "Gad Dam," then decided that tradition would have to be put aside at least this once. Summersville, the second closest town, got the honor.

Summersville is the largest of five man-made lakes that each year attract thousands of visitors to the West Virginia Heartland for summer fun — whether it's fishing, camping, boating, water skiing or just plain relaxing. But the region is more than a summertime playground. Heartland residents take their heritage and history seriously and work hard to keep it alive through an impressive calender of yearly fairs and festivals.

The Heartland comprises all or part of 10 counties — Upshur, Lewis, Gilmer, Calhoun, Roane, Clay, Nicholas, Webster, Braxton and Randolph. As a region, it's short on bright lights and big-city thrills. Instead, it's made up of countless small towns, wooded hillsides, green meadows and mountain streams. Many of its people make their living from the land — farming, mining or timbering. The region is also home to several small colleges, both public and private.

In years past, the Heartland counties were isolated from the rest of West Virginia but today they are served by a network of modern roads. Interstate 79 bisects the region down the middle, and U.S. 19 provides easy access from the south. The region's lakes make it a prime recreational area, and modern highways make those lakes easy for people to visit and enjoy.

In the years following World War II, when the Corps of Engineers began constructing its far-flung network of flood-control dams and reservoirs, the Corps anticipated the new projects would attract many fun-seekers but failed to foresee just how enormous their recreational appeal would be. Post-war Americans — with more leisure time, more money and more cars than their parents — flocked to the new reservoirs.

By the 1970s, recreational use of Corps projects was growing at a pace three times the annual increase in the Gross National Product and six times faster than the rate of population growth. Little wonder that the very word "reservoir" was stricken from the Corps' official vocabulary. Instead, the water projects now are called "lakes," in recognition

Swimmers enjoy the rugged cliffs and calm waters of Summersville Lake (left), while rafters (center) prefer the rushing excitement below the dam. The Gauley River below Summersville Dam provides some of the nation's best whitewater, as the adventurers running Pillow Rock Rapid (bottom) will attest.

of their important recreational role.

Summersville Lake, the southernmost of the Heartland's lakes, is a perfect example. President Lyndon B. Johnson dedicated Summersville on September 3, 1966, saying: "We have come here to consumate an act of faith in the future of West Virginia." Since then, Summersville has become a tourist mecca. Impounded behind one of the world's largest earthen dams (390 feet high and 2,280 feet long), the lake boasts more than 60 twisting miles of shoreline. Its expanses of flat water are great for water skiing, windsurfing and sailing. Sheer sandstone cliffs rise high above

WEST VIRGINIA STATE ARCHIVES

▲ GERALD S. RATLIFF ▼

Jackson's Mill provided the boyhood home of Thomas J. "Stonewall" Jackson. The Confederate hero's statue (top right) now graces the courthouse grounds in Clarksburg.

the lake and, below the surface, scuba divers explore its crystal clear waters. Cold and deep, the mountain lake challenges anglers who fish for smallmouth bass in summer and for walleye in winter and early spring.

The estimated annual number of visitors to Summersville Lake is one and a half million and growing.

At the northern end of the region in Lewis County near Weston is Stonewall Jackson Lake, named for the famed Confederate general. (More about Jackson, one of West Virginia's best-known native sons, later.) Much of the land the federal government acquired for the project has been leased to the

state for recreation use. Stonewall Jackson State Park offers facilities for water sports, camping and hiking. And a far-larger adjacent tract is managed as a public fishing and hunting area.

A 45-passenger paddlewheel pontoon boat, the *Stonewall Jackson*, offers sight-seeing, dinner and charter cruises. Outfitted with fake smokestacks, the boat is a credible imitation of an old-time steamboat. As the paddlewheeler floats along, the captain points out sites of historic interest and key natural features. Passengers also get a close-up look at a variety of wildlife — deer, turkey, fox, beaver, raccoon and maybe

Churchgoers at the Bulltown historical complex recall the upright living of early times.

The wooded valley of the Gauley (left) was not spared Civil War violence. The Battle of Carnifex Ferry is recreated annually (bottom left), while artillery stands permanent watch at Carnifex Ferry Battlefield State Park.

▲ GERALD S. RATLIFF ▼

even a bear.

Braxton County is home to not one but two man-made lakes, with adjoining wildlife management areas for fishing and hunting — Burnsville Lake and Sutton Lake. Like Stonewall Jackson Lake, both are handy to Interstate 79.

Stonecoal Dam was constructed by the Allegheny Power System on the Right Fork of Stonecoal Creek, five miles east of Weston in Lewis County. Stonecoal Lake has a 10-horsepower limit for outboard motors. As a result, recreational

boaters other than fishermen are few. If peace and quiet are what you're looking for, you'll find it here.

If, on the other hand, it's heritage and history you seek, there's also plenty of it in this section of the Mountain State.

About the time Thomas Jefferson was building his beloved Monticello at Charlottesville, hardy pioneers were establishing themselves across the mountains in what's now the West Virginia Heartland. Among the first arrivals were two brothers, John and

Samuel Pringle, who in 1761, deserted Fort Pitt in Pennsylvania and traveled to what is now the town of Buckhannon in Upshur County. There they set up housekeeping in a hollow sycamore tree. When they ran out of provisions, one of the brothers ventured back to civilization, where he told everyone about the plentiful game, wild fruits and fertile land he and his brother had found. The British had forbidden anyone from settling "across the mountains," but the lure was too great to be ignored. Soon, small parties of adventuresome settlers began making their way to the Heartland.

Early arrivals included

John Hacker, Thomas and Jesse Hughes, and John Jackson, with his sons Edward and George. John Hacker's cabin, built circa 1768-69, is still standing on the road that runs between Berlin and Jane Lew in Lewis County. Jesse Hughes settled across from what is now the Wilderness Plantation Inn, off Interstate 79 at Jane Lew.

Though Indians didn't make permanent homes in the Heartland during the time of white exploration and settlement, they used the area for hunting. Legend has it that famed Indian chief Tecumseh was born not far from where John Hacker built his cabin. Not surprisingly, the Indians

▲ DAVID E. FATTALEH ▼

The West Virginia State Wildlife Center

The West Virginia State Wildlife Center is located in Upshur County about 12 miles south of Buckhannon on State Route 20. It boasts an impressive collection of animals, all of which have something important in common — they all are, or have been, native to the state.

Visit the center and you'll see bison, deer, cougar, fox, bear, skunk, possum, raccoon and other four-legged residents. The center's collection of birds includes eagles, owls and ring-necked pheasants.

For many years, this facility was called the French Creek Game Farm. More than the name has changed. The old displays were developed piecemeal over a half century and were badly antiquated. So, beginning in 1984, a new exhibit area was designed and built. Animals are not

resented the growing number of settlers and clashes between the two were frequent and bloody. The resulting bloodshed was recounted in Alexander Scott Withers' classic *Chronicles of Border Warfare*, published at Clarksburg in 1831.

Weston, the county seat of Lewis County, was established in 1818. Its name was changed to Flesherville in 1819 and to Weston later the same year. The origin of the latter name has been lost. Weston first grew as a center of commerce on the east-west Staunton to Parkersburg Turnpike, now U.S. 33, and boomed shortly before the Civil War when oil and gas were discovered nearby. Evidence of

the town's post-Civil War prosperity can be seen in its ornate late Victorian architecture.

In 1858, the State of Virginia authorized the building of a mental hospital at Weston but construction was delayed during the Civil War. With the creation of West Virginia in 1863, ownership of the uncompleted hospital passed to the new state. The hospital — said to be the largest hand-cut stone building in the nation — finally was completed and opened in 1864. For more than 100 years, it would be the state's largest mental hospital, at one time housing as many as 2,500 patients. Virtually self-sufficient, the huge hospital had a farm

The West Virginia Wildlife Center harbors animal species native to the Mountain State.

confined to cages but in pens designed to make them feel more at home. All have sheds or other structures they can take shelter in when the weather turns bad — or when they're tired of having people stare at them.

The Left Fork of Holly River (top) tumbles through Webster County, while the Cranberry makes its slower way among boulders and maple trees.

A rusting oil derrick still holds its place in the hills of Clay County.

where much of its food was grown, a reservoir, living quarters for its staff, even its own mine where coal for heating was dug.

In recent years, treatment of the mentally ill has undergone a dramatic change. Many patients who previously would have been institutionalized in a large hospital now are treated at smaller facilities in their own communities, where they can be near family or friends. The old Weston State Hospital was vacated in May of 1994.

In 1829, the growing number of residents in the vicinity and the natural importance of the site as a center for the Hacker's Creek community led Lewis Maxwell, one of Weston's founders, to purchase the nearby Jacob Bennett farm and, in 1835, to divide it into lots. The town thus laid out was named Jane Lew in honor of Jane Lewis, Maxwell's mother. Today, visitors to Weston and Jane Lew can shop for antiques, basketry, hand-made glass or other West Virginia treasures at a variety of shops.

Not far from Weston is Jackson's Mill, the boyhood home of General Thomas Jonathan Jackson — known to history as "Stonewall."

Jackson was born January 21, 1824, in Clarksburg. His father and mother died while he was quite young, and the boy

Helvetia

Every West Virginia town has a tale to tell, but few as unusual as that of Helvetia, a community of 150 or so people in Randolph County.

Helvetia — pronounced hel-VEE-shah —

DAVID E. FATTALEH

The charm of Helvetia is manifested in its homes and shops and in such details as the stained-glass church window. The old haymaking photograph, by Helvetian Walter Aegerter, portrays the hard work which built the community.

was settled by Swiss immigrants in the late 1860's. The story of their trek from Switzerland, to Brooklyn, New York, to Clarksburg and, finally, to Randolph County has been told and retold over the years and, as often happens, has taken on several variations.

One local legend has it that when the settlers' train arrived in Clarksburg they were met by a land agent who had lured them to West Virginia with tales of a thriving Swiss community in the hills. But when the Swiss arrived at what they had expected to be an established town, they found nothing but wilderness. Some were discouraged, but others stayed and built Helvetia, a West Virginia town with little touches of the Swiss here and there. Blood from these hardy first settlers still runs through many families who live in and around Helvetia.

In recent years, local residents, aware that their town's unique character was slipping away, have been working hard to capture and preserve it. Many of the buildings have been restored. If you visit, don't miss the log cabin Helvetia Museum and the Zion Presbyterian Church, originally the Helvetia German Evangelical Reformed Church, built in 1882.

During the second weekend of each September, the Helvetia

Fair entertains visitors with folk dancing, demonstrations, exhibits, arts, crafts, and, of course, tasty Swiss food. Visitors are assured: "You'll never go hungry in Helvetia."

DAVID E. FATTALEH

WEST VIRGINIA STATE ARCHIVES

grew up with relatives at nearby Jackson's Mill. Settlers in western Virginia didn't have the luxury of a grocery store where they could go to buy their staples. Homegrown corn and wheat supplied the cornmeal and wheat flour the pioneers needed. Small grist mills processed the corn and wheat, and it was at such a mill that Jackson worked as a boy.

The future general had little formal education, and when he won an appointment to the U.S. Military Academy at West Point, he had to struggle to keep up with his classmates. But he persevered, graduating 17th in his class. Commissioned a second lieutenant in the artillery, he

The crowning of Queen Sylvia is a highlight of the Forest Festival.

West Virginia's logging heritage shows its competitive side in sawing (above) and tree-chopping (left) contests at the Mountain State Forest Festival in Elkins.

joined his regiment in Mexico, where the United States was then at war. He served there with distinction. Finding the peacetime army tedious and unrewarding, he resigned and took a teaching post at Virginia Military Institute in Lexington, Virginia. At the outbreak of the Civil War, he volunteered his services to the Confederacy.

On July 21, 1861, Jackson was in command of a brigade during the First Battle of Manassas (Bull Run). Confederate General Bernard Bee, trying to rally his faltering men, saw Jackson and his brigade holding fast and shouted, "There stands Jackson's brigade like a stone wall! Rally behind the Virgin-ians!" From that time on, Jackson was known to one and all as "Stonewall."

Perhaps the ablest of Robert E. Lee's generals, Jackson played an important role in many Civil War battles. He may have been a mediocre student at West Point but today he's looked on as one of the finest tacticians in military history. When Lee divided his army into two corps, he gave General James Longstreet command of the first corps and awarded Jackson the second. On the evening of May 2, 1863, as Jackson rode in the gathering dusk, he was mistakenly shot by one of his own men and mortally wounded. He lingered for days, dying on May 10. His death left a

Elegance on Campus

The names of Henry Gassaway Davis and his son-in-law, Stephen Benton Elkins, are written large in West Virginia history and on the state's landscape. Both have towns named after them — Davis in Tucker County and Elkins in Randolph County. And their two names are linked in Davis and Elkins College in Elkins.

Davis and Elkins College grew out of a missionary effort by Virginia's Presbyterian Church to provide educational opportunities in the mountain areas of the new state of West

banks and other enterprises.

Halliehurst is a true Victorian showplace, complete with six bathrooms and an elegant third-floor ballroom. Its "Pullman Room" features arched beams, imitating the look of a railroad coach of the period. In a museum off the main ballroom, the Darby Collection showcases an outstanding variety of early American artifacts.

Graceland Mansion, another Elkins historic site, was completed in 1893 by Davis. A native of Baltimore, Davis was a station agent for the Baltimore & Ohio Railroad at Piedmont in Mineral County when the Civil War began. Using his connections in the railroad, he made a fortune selling supplies to the Union Army. He later turned to politics and served 12 years in the Senate. At this writing, Graceland is being restored for use as an inn, to be operated in conjunction with the college's hospitality management program.

The Davis Memorial Presbyterian Church and the Randolph County Courthouse and Jail are other historic Elkins structures. Both are open for public viewing.

The spirit of the benefactors lives on at Davis and Elkins College, in Stephen Benton Elkins's mansion (right) and the statue of Henry Gassaway Davis.

DAVID E. FATTALEH

void in the Confederate ranks that was never filled.

In the 1920's, the family farm where Jackson grew up became a 4-H campground, the first of its kind. Today, Jackson's Mill is a 523-acre, year-round conference center. It features a historical district that includes the old grist mill, now a museum. The original mill was last used in the 1890s. But in recent years another mill, built in Greenbrier County in 1794, was moved to Jackson's Mill and restored to operating condition. Lucky visitors often find it busily grinding away.

Each Labor Day weekend, Jackson's Mill is the focus of the Stonewall Jackson Heritage Arts

Virginia in the years following the Civil War. The effort met with only limited success until 1901 when Davis and Elkins jointly donated a tract of land and $30,000 to found a college for resident West Virginia Presbyterians. The school began operation in 1904.

Today, a centerpiece of the Davis and Elkins campus is Halliehurst Mansion, the restored summer home of Elkins, who was Secretary of War under President Benjamin Harrison, later served in the U.S. Senate and, with his father-in-law, was a partner in a bewildering array of West Virginia mining companies, railroads,

GERALD S. RATLIFF

West Virginia Wesleyan (left) and
Alderson-Broaddus College (above)
are among the colleges of the
Heartland counties.

and Crafts Jubilee. The Jubilee is one of more than a dozen fairs and festivals that celebrate the heart of West Virginia's culture, logically enough, in the Heartland. The Jackson's Mill festival features a crafts show and sale, lots of music, down-home cooking and a Civil War re-enactment.

Two of the most respected festivals celebrated in the Heartland are found in college towns — the West Virginia State Folk Festival in Glenville, home of Glenville State College, and the Augusta Heritage Festival, held on the Davis and Elkins College campus in Elkins.

The State Folk Festival, scheduled on the third weekend in June each year, began in 1950 as the brainchild of Dr. Patrick Gainer, as an outgrowth of courses in Appalachian culture he was teaching at Glenville. Gainer later left to join the faculty at West Virginia University but his festival kept right on going. The emphasis at the State Folk Festival is on authenticity. As one long-time participant, explains: "It's a family-oriented event and that's the way we try to keep it. There have been attempts to bring in commercial music ... but we try to honor West Virginia musicians who keep the faith by keeping the traditional ways."

Each summer, the Augusta Heritage Center at Davis and Elkins College offers five weeks of intensive workshops in traditional music, dance and crafts. Since its inception in 1972, the Augusta program has grown into the largest of its kind in the country and has become a major factor in the cultural and economic life of Elkins and Randolph County. Augusta Director Margo Blevin estimates that the economic impact of the 1995 edition was more than $1.5 million. Some 2,700 participants came from 46 states and 16 foreign countries. The Augusta Heritage Festival, the annual program's traditional three-day finale, attracted an estimated 5,000 additional people to Elkins City Park and the D&E

campus for concerts, a craft fair and various family activities.

Elkins also is home to the Mountain State Forest Festival, conducted each October when the region's woodlands turn yellow and gold. The Forest Festival originated in 1930 as a homecoming celebration for Randolph Countians but quickly began to attract visitors other than those with local roots. Over the years, all manner of events, from a tree-felling contest to a 10-K run, have been part of the festival, but the centerpiece has never changed — the coronation of a forest queen and her court. From the very first festival, the annual celebration has emphasized the scenic beauty of West

Old-time mountain music captures the heart of the West Virginia Heartland. These musicians play at the Stonewall Jackson Jubilee (right) and at the State Folk Festival at Glenville (below right and below).

LARRY BELCHER

STEPHEN J. SHALUTA, JR. ▲

Virginia's woodlands and the need for conserving the state's forests and streams.

Buckhannon, the home of West Virginia Wesleyan College, is the scene of the yearly Strawberry Festival, a springtime bash honoring the tasty red berry. High school bands march down Strawberry Lane, competing for scholarships, as youngsters flock to the perennial carnival and their parents take in the arts and crafts exhibits or maybe marvel at the antique cars on display.

The last weekend in June brings the Bluegrass-Country Music Festival at Summersville,

which each year attracts some of the biggest names in bluegrass music. The festival began in 1981, when organizers Edgar and Eunice Kitchen sent out flyers announcing a five-band program. They were hoping for a big turnout. What they got, they laughingly recall, was 98 adults, a boy and his dog. But the event has grown rapidly since and now draws bluegrass fans across the country and around the world.

Huntington is West Virginia's biggest Ohio River city.

Opposite Page - Ritter Park brings the attractions of the countryside into town.

River City Region

CHAPTER 5

Railroads played a crucial role in shaping West Virginia. When the Baltimore & Ohio reached Wheeling in 1853 it helped make that city a gateway to the west. At the same time, points along the B&O, notably Grafton and Fairmont, became busy railroad towns. The Ohio River Railroad, completed from Wheeling to Point Pleasant in 1884, gave the state its first north-south railroad. And the years 1884 to 1890 saw the tracks of the Norfolk & Western Railway slowly make their way across southern West Virginia, where they tapped that region's rich coal deposits.

But nowhere did railroad-ing have a greater impact than in Huntington, for it was rail tycoon Collis P. Huntington (1822-1900) who created the city, causing it to be built on a vacant tract of river bottom.

Collis P. Huntington's remarkable career resembled the rags-to-riches stories popularized in the Horatio Alger novels of his day. As a young man, he started out in business as a Yankee peddler, walking from farm to farm, selling whatever merchan-dise he could carry on his back. When he died, he was worth approximately $70 million. Huntington made his first fortune in California, where he joined the gold rush of 1849, not as a miner but a merchant,

selling pickaxes, shovels and other items to the eager miners. In 1855, he teamed up with fellow Californians Mark Hopkins, Charles Crocker and Leland Stanford to build what would become the Central Pacific, the western half of the long-dreamed-of transcontinental railroad. The Central Pacific laid its tracks eastward and its rival, the Union Pacific, headed west. The two sets of tracks met at Promontory Point, Utah, and there, on May 10, 1869, officials drove a symbolic golden spike uniting the continent.

The echoes of that spike-driving had hardly died away when a delegation representing the Chesapeake & Ohio Railway

called on Huntington, imploring him to buy a controlling interest in the eastern railroad. Hunting-ton at first resisted but eventu-ally agreed.

Americans long had dreamed of linking the James River and the Ohio River. Once the idea of doing it by canal had proven impractical, the James River and Kanawha Turnpike was built. The C&O's predecessors had made a bold effort at linking the rivers by rail, but the Civil War had intervened. Locomotives and rolling stock had been destroyed, as had much of the track.

Huntington knew that if the C&O was to survive, much less prosper, its tracks must

Hard-working railroaders (above) built and maintained the tracks which gave life to the regional economy. Trains (left) have been a part of Huntington from the first.

A statue of founder Collis P. Huntington claims a place of honor at the city's Heritage Village.

quickly be pushed to the Ohio, where freight and passengers could readily be transferred to steamboats for the trip on to Cincinnati and other points downriver. In the summer of 1869, he set out to explore the C&O's proposed route to the Ohio. Several locations had been suggested for the railroad's western terminus, among them the village of Guyandotte, a popular overnight stop on the James River and Kanawha Turnpike. After exploring the area thoroughly, Huntington instead picked a site a mile or so downstream, just where the Big Sandy flows into the Ohio.

Local legend holds that Huntington's decision was based as much on personal pique as on logic. As the story goes, when the inspection party arrived in Guyandotte, the travelers tied their horses to a hitching post and entered an inn. While Huntington was inside, his horse managed to climb up on the crude wooden boardwalk in front of the inn, blocking the way. At this point, Guyandotte's mayor came along, marched into the inn and demanded that the horse's owner identify himself. Huntington came forward, the mayor fined him $5 on the spot, and the next day the citizens of Guyandotte were sorely disappointed to learn that their village was not to be the C&O's western terminus.

53620 Ohio River Scene, Huntington, W Va.

River boats were Huntington's other means of travel, before the coming of improved roadways.

The distinctive 31st Street suspension bridge is a modern city landmark.

Huntington placed his brother-in-law, Colonel Delos W. Emmons, in charge of procuring the necessary land. Soon Emmons had purchased 21 farms, a total of nearly 5,000 acres. Much of it was reserved by the railroad for right of way, extensive machine and car shops, engine houses, a depot and other necessary buildings. The remainder was divided into lots for resale. Huntington hired Rufus Cook, a Boston surveyor, to lay out his new town. Today, the city is known for its broad avenues and handy intersecting streets. That was no happy accident but a direct result of Huntington's detailed instructions to Cook.

On February 27, 1871, the West Virginia Legislature approved an act incorporating the new city. A locomotive was floated down the Ohio by barge, and a construction crew began laying track eastward from Huntington. Another crew pushed westward from Richmond. The two crews met at Hawk's Nest on January 29, 1873, and a gala first train arrived in Huntington from Richmond, carrying a number of guests and a demijohn of water from the James River which was emptied with due pomp into the Ohio. On the train's return trip, the same demijohn carried water from the Ohio to the James to complete the symbolic gesture.

COURT HOUSE SQUARE AND FOURTH AVENUE, HUNTINGTON, W. VA.

The Cabell County Courthouse (above and left) has occupied a prominent downtown square since Huntington's early days.

The Arcade, on Huntington's 4th Avenue, recalls merchandising styles of an earlier era and embodies the city's commercial heritage.

The eastbound train also handled something far more vital to the future of the railroad and the new city it served — four carloads of West Virginia coal. Coal soon moved westward as well, traveling to the city by the new railroad, then being loaded onto river barges for towboats to push up or down the Ohio.

This linkage of river and rail transport is a central theme in the city's history. The C&O's tracks made Huntington a vital shipping point. Coal dug from the mines of southern West Virginia was sent to market via Huntington, and a steady stream of manufactured goods flowed through the city to customers in the coalfields.

Moreover, the site Collis P. Huntington chose proved an ideal spot to build a town. Not only was it well served by river and rail, it was near the raw materials that industry needed — not just coal but natural gas, oil, timber, sand for making glass and clay for fashioning brick. Little wonder that businesses soon flocked to the new city.

In a spirited 1887 election, Huntington supplanted Barboursville as the county seat of Cabell County. The county government was moved the next year and initially shared a two-story brick building with City Hall. Huntington's boundaries were extended in 1909 to take in Central City, a rival municipality

Chuck Yeager

"His name is Chuck Yeager," wrote novelist Tom Wolfe. "He was the first man to break the sound barrier, and he is the quintessence of 'the right stuff' — the secret code of the very best and bravest pilots."

Shucks, says Yeager, it wasn't a case of the right stuff. Just dumb luck. "It's more meaningful to be in the right place at the right time," he insists. But, despite the famed pilot's protests, it takes more than luck for a country boy from West Virginia to become an aviation legend.

Chuck Yeager was born February 13, 1923, at Myra — "a few farmhouses, a post office and a country store" — in Lincoln County. The family soon moved to nearby Hamlin, where Yeager went to school. He was far happier hunting or fishing than sitting in a classroom. He did well in any subject requiring math, he recalls, "but my English and history teachers had to search for excuses to pass me."

His diploma from Hamlin High School in hand, an 18-year-old Yeager joined the Army Air Corps in September 1941. He became an airplane mechanic but volunteered for pilot training. On his first flight, he threw up all over the cockpit. Undeterred, he earned his pilot wings in 1943 and was sent to England to fly the P-51 Mustang fighter.

In 64 World War II combat missions, the young Lincoln Countian became a "double ace," shooting down 13 German planes — five on one mission. Among his kills was one of Germany's first jet

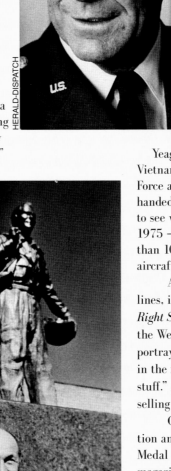

fighters. On March 5, 1944, he was shot down over occupied France but escaped capture when elements of the French Resistance helped him reach the Spanish border.

After the war, Yeager became a test pilot at Wright-Patterson Air Force Base in Dayton, Ohio. On October 14, 1947, at Muroc Dry Lake Air Field (now Edwards Air Force Base) in California, he won his place in history when he rocketed the Bell X-1 plane past the speed of sound — despite two cracked ribs from a riding accident a few days before. Nobody knew what would happen when the X-1 neared the sound barrier. Some were sure the plane would shake itself to pieces. Instead, Yeager found it "smooth as a baby's bottom. ... There should have been a bump on the road, something to let you know you had just punched a hole in the sound barrier."

Yeager later flew combat missions in both the Korean and Vietnam wars and carried out a challenging list of other Air Force assignments. When a defecting North Korean pilot handed over a Russian MIG 15, it was Yeager who took it up to see what it could do. When he retired from active duty in 1975 — by this time a brigadier general — he had logged more than 10,000 hours of flying time in 180 different military aircraft.

Although Yeager's 1947 flight made worldwide headlines, it was Wolfe's book about the U.S. space program, *The Right Stuff*, and the hit movie made from it, that transformed the West Virginia pilot into a nationally known figure. Wolfe portrayed Yeager as courageous, calm, detached, even laconic in the face of great danger — a true possessor of "the right stuff." And the 1985 publication of *Yeager*, the general's best-selling autobiography, won him still more fans.

Chuck Yeager has won virtually every military decoration and aviation award possible, including a special peacetime Medal Of Honor. His picture has been on the cover of *Time* magazine. His TV commercials have made his face familiar to millions.

And West Virginia has honored its native son. Charleston today is served by Yeager Airport. In Huntington, Marshall University each year inducts talented high school students into its Society of Yeager Scholars. And in front of Hamlin High stands a life-sized bronze statue of, to borrow Yeager's own phrase, "the guy who broke the sound barrier."

14783—3rd Avenue looking East from 9th Street, Huntington, W. Va.

The historic district, as evening falls.

Huntington's wide streets were built to serve places of business and places of worship.

to the west, and again in 1911, to absorb Guyandotte on the east.

The first years of the 20th century saw the construction of several public buildings that still grace the city's downtown. The present Cabell County Court-house was built in 1901, with wings added in 1924 and 1940. Steel tycoon and philanthropist Andrew Carnegie gave the city a handsome public library. Opened in 1903, it now houses the Huntington Junior College of Business, while the Cabell County Pubic Library is located in a modern building just across 9th Street. A fine new post office (now the Sidney L. Christie Federal Building) was built in 1909. And 1912 brought construction of Huntington City Hall, at a cost of $115,300 — a bargain even then.

Rufus Cook's original plan made no provision for a public park. In 1908, under Mayor Rufus Switzer, the city purchased 55 acres of land on Four Pole Creek as the site of a new incinerator. Not surprisingly, nearby residents protested. Switzer relented and suggested using the tract as a park instead. Businessman C. L. Ritter, in consideration of the city building a road along his estate, donated additional acreage and the new park was named for him. Ritter Park, dedicated in 1913, is one of the city's grandest jewels. The park includes a popular walking-

Amazing Glass

There is no material more amazing than glass — and no manufacturing process more demanding. In an age that glorifies the machine, the skill of the glassblower remains a challenge to time.

The Huntington area is home to not one but two world-famous makers of art glass — Blenko Glass Company in Milton and Pilgrim Glass Corporation in Ceredo.

Blenko began in 1895 as a maker of blown sheet glass and stained glass. Today, Richard Blenko, great-grandson of the company's British-born founder, William J. Blenko, carries on the family tradition of fine glass.

Its richly colored glass, treasured worldwide, can be seen in windows at Colonial Williamsburg, Washington Cathedral, the U.S. Air Force Academy, and the Riyadh Airport in Saudi Arabia. Each year, Blenko crafts the Country Music Awards presented to the winning singers and musicians in the county music industry. And hand-blown Blenko glassware can be found on many of the nation's finest tables.

Pilgrim was established by business-man Alfred E. Knobler in 1949, when he persuaded the town of Ceredo to pipe in the natural gas necessary to fire the new company's furnaces.

Pilgrim is known to glass lovers the world over for its fine line of cranberry glass — the vivid color is achieved

by fusing solid gold with lead crystal — and its sand-carved cameo glass. The latter is made by layering colors of glass one on another and then carving a design into the top layer. Although prices for cameo pieces begin at about $100 they range as high as $3,000 for a numbered or signed edition.

Both Blenko and Pilgrim offer factory tours and feature gift shops with bargain-priced "seconds." Blenko also has an interesting museum.

Not surprisingly, the Huntington Museum of Art boasts one of the finest glassware collections in the nation. The collection chronicles the historic ebb and flow of glassmaking throughout the Ohio Valley and includes pieces from many long-closed factories. It includes early pressed, cut and Victorian art glass as well as impressive examples of contemporary American studio glass.

The Huntington region is one of America's most important glassmaking areas. Workers (above and right) produce glass and glass molds at Blenko. Pilgrim Glass is famous for its sand-carved cameo glass (top).

DAVID E. FATTALEH

STEPHEN J. SHALUTA, JR.

The Keith-Albee (below) has provided entertainment since vaudeville times, while Heritage Station (left) recreates the atmosphere of railroad days.

Huntington offers the amenities of modern business life, as well as its own rich heritage.

jogging trail, a handsome rose garden, tennis courts, an amphitheater and an award-winning children's playground.

Huntington's economy continued to expand after World War I, and the downtown saw another building boom, the results of which still can be seen. The Central Huntington Garage, opened in 1927, offered indoor parking, auto maintenance, car washing and even uniformed chauffeur service. On May 8, 1928, Huntington theater owners A. B. and S. J. Hyman opened their lavish Keith-Albee Theater. The $2 million, 3,000-seat movie palace boasted 19 red-uniformed ushers, a ceiling studded with artificial clouds and stars, an eight-piece orchestra and, of course, a mighty Wurlitzer organ. The uniformed chauffeurs and ushers may be gone, but today you can still park your car at the Central Huntington Garage, then stroll to the nearby Keith to take in a movie.

Huntington was one of many Ohio River communities that, in the wake of the 1937 flood, built high floodwalls, retreated behind them and then more or less forgot about the

Postcard view of Ritter Park (above) and a recent view of the park in springtime.

river locked away on the other side. In Huntington, an urban renewal project was the impetus for clearing the riverbank of its assorted junk and "hobo jungle," and transforming it into a handsome park. Opened in 1984, David W. Harris Riverfront Park — named for Huntington's veteran urban renewal director — has proved so popular the city is undertaking an expansion that will double its size.

Not far from Harris Park is Heritage Village, formed from the city's former Baltimore & Ohio Railroad passenger and freight depots. (The B&O took over the old Ohio River Railroad, after it had pushed its tracks on down the Ohio from Point Pleasant to Huntington.) The complex, popular with out-of-town visitors and local residents alike, includes The Station, a Victorian-style restaurant; various shops; a vintage steam locomotive, and a restored Pullman car. Local lore has it that the old Bank of Huntington, moved to the village from its original 3rd Avenue site, was the scene of an 1875 robbery by the infamous Jesse James gang.

Drive up Eighth Street Hill from Ritter Park and you'll find the Huntington Museum of Art, one of the city's premier attractions. Opened in 1952, it is West Virginia's largest art museum, providing residents and visitors access to distinguished

Old Main (left) is the historic center of Marshall University, and Memorial Student Center (below) is the cornerstone of student life. Thundering Herd football (above) holds the central place in the heart of many fans.

collections, outstanding exhibitions and nationally acclaimed educational programs. A 1970 addition — designed by famed Bauhaus architect Walter Gropius — doubled the museum's size.

Today, 125 years after its founding, Huntington, like many cities, has seen a sharp decline in its once-proud industrial ranks and, since construction of the Huntington Mall in nearby Barboursville, its downtown no longer is the region's unchallenged retail center. Nonetheless, the city is thriving, with a handsome — and busy — business district. Much of the downtown's recovery has been sparked by the "Huntington Main Street" program. A low-interest loan pool

The Huntington Museum of Art is among the region's most distinguished institutions.

established by Main Street in cooperation with local banks and city government has enabled property owners to undertake 55 rehabilitation projects representing more than $3.7 million.

With 12,500 students and more than 600 faculty members, Marshall University is a key element in virtually every aspect of today's Huntington. Certainly it is now the city's leading "industry," pumping more than $300 million a year into the local economy.

Marshall traces its start to the year 1837 when the citizens of Guyandotte and the surrounding farm country decided they needed a school. They met at the home of John Laidley, who

The Z. D. Ramsdell House

Just west of Huntington on U.S. 60 is Ceredo, a proud community that can trace its roots directly to the nation's historic struggle over slavery. In recent years, local residents have painstakingly restored the Z. D. Ramsdell house as a visible symbol of that heritage.

In 1857, most of Ceredo was farmland owned by Thomas Jordan. But that year saw Thomas Thayer, a Massachusetts congressman and outspoken abolitionist, borrow money from fellow abolitionist Charles Hoard, a New York businessman, to purchase a large portion of Jordan's farm.

There, Thayer established a new town, naming it after Ceres, the Greek goddess of grain and harvest, because of the agricultural opportunities he foresaw. The settlement, Thayer decreed, would be slave-free. Several New England families migrated to the new town and started businesses — a sawmill, a glass works and a match factory. When the Civil War erupted, Thomas Thayer was forced into bankruptcy.

One of Ceredo's first settlers was Zopher D. Ramsdell, a bootmaker from Maine, who in 1858 built a handsome two-story brick house on B Street. During the war, Ceredo was the site of Camp Pierpont, the headquarters for Company B of the 5th Regiment of West Virginia's Volunteer Infantry, and Ramsdell was company quartermaster. After the war, he became Ceredo's first postmaster.

Local stories say that in the years before the war, the Ramsdell house was a stop on the Underground Railroad, which smuggled fugitive slaves from the South to the North. As part of Virginia, West Virginia was slave territory, while Ohio, just across the Ohio River, was a free state.

It is said that Ramsdell hid slaves in the attic of his house and then smuggled them through a tunnel that led from the basement to the riverbank — and freedom.

The Ramsdell House occupies a spot in the westernmost part of West Virginia.

Riverfront fireworks and a busy schedule of cultural affairs brighten life in Huntington.

assumed leadership of the project and named the new school Marshall Academy in honor of his friend, the late Chief Justice John Marshall. The school began in a log cabin. Laidley and his fellow trustees purchased the cabin and the 1.25-acre plot of land where it stood. The price: $40. That land is now the site of Marshall's landmark building, Old Main.

In 1858, Marshall Academy was renamed Marshall College, but the coming of the Civil War soon forced it to close its doors. In 1867, Cabell County voters approved a $5,000 tax levy to reopen Marshall as a state normal school to train teachers. But until 1912, Marshall remained a secondary school. It wasn't until that year that freshman and sophomore college classes were added, and it would be 1920 before it was a true four-year college.

On the eve of World War II, Marshall had 2,000 students. The post-war era, when returning GIs flooded the campus, saw spectacular growth and the claiming of university status in 1961. Recent additions to the 60-acre campus adjacent to downtown Huntington include a 30,000-seat football stadium and a multi-million dollar fine and performing arts center. And the Marshall School of Medicine is pacing the city's dramatic growth as a regional medical center.

The Huntington Civic Arena offers dynamic events each season.

The Pumpkin Festival at Milton celebrates local rural heritage.

Since its inception in 1937, the Marshall Artists Series has brought countless nationally and internationally known artists to Huntington to perform on the stage of the Keith-Albee for audiences of students and townspeople.

Marshall President J. Wade Gilley first came to Huntington in 1991, when he was interviewing for the post he now holds. Today, when he recruits people to join Marshall's faculty or staff, he wants them to see the area where they could live.

"I came up with a list of eight or 10 things that are really impressive for me. Then I try to send them off to see two or three things," he says. Gilly's list

includes Huntington's wide streets, its hospitals, Harris Riverfront Park, Ritter Park and the Huntington Museum of Art. "People are friendly and helpful," he says. "One thing I've found is that if we get local people showing them around, they are very impressed with how friendly and open Huntingtonians are."

Huntington, with about 55,000 people, is the largest city in a four-county area known as the Tri-State. The region includes not just Cabell and Wayne counties in West Virginia, but also Boyd County, just across the Big Sandy in Kentucky, and Lawrence County in Ohio. Together, the four counties

number about 288,000 people.

Cabell County is also home to two incorporated towns, very much communities of their own and not just suburbs of Huntington.

Indians hunting the area's plentiful game and digging for salt at Salt Rock were the early inhabitants of the Barboursville area. In 1813, an act of the Virginia General Assembly established Barboursville as a village of 339 people. It was a center of commerce and political activity until the coming of the C&O to Huntington. It served as the county seat until 1888, when the records, ledgers and books were removed to Huntington. Today, Huntington may have the

Cabell County Courthouse but Barboursville has the Huntington Mall, West Virginia's largest.

The town of Milton was incorporated by the West Virginia Legislature on September 6, 1876. Earlier that same year, a covered bridge was built to provide access to the town from the James River and Kanawha Turnpike. The bridge still stands, as does the nearby Union Baptist Church, which was organized in 1810 and occupied by Union troops during the Civil War. Milton is the scene each October of the "West Virginia Pumpkin Festival," with arts and crafts, music, pumpkin delicacies and a pumpkin weighing contest — with a 200-pound minimum!

A coal preparation plant at the McDowell County town of Keystone.

Opposite Page - Pinnacle Rock State Park marks the eastern boundary of the southern coalfields.

Southern Coal Country

CHAPTER 6

Found in all but two of West Virginia's 55 counties, coal has been mined here for well over a century. But in the years prior to the Civil War most of the Mountain State's coal was consumed within a few miles of the mine mouth.

In the early 1800s, coal supplanted wood as the fuel at the salt furnaces of the Kanawha Valley. Northern Panhandle coal went to feed the ironworks, foundaries, glass factories and other enterprises of the Wheeling area. Most of the limited amount of coal mined east of the Alleghenies was shipped down the Potomac to Harper's Ferry, with some going on to

Georgetown and Baltimore. As late as 1880, the state's total coal production was only 1.5 million tons a year. What was missing in the early years was a cheap method of transportation to get the coal from mine to market. The coming of the railroads provided that missing link — and changed West Virginia forever.

The Baltimore & Ohio Railroad, whose tracks reached Wheeling in 1853 and stretched on to Parkersburg in 1857, and the Chesapeake & Ohio Railway, which ran its first train from Richmond to Huntington in 1873, were the first railroads to traverse the state. Neither was built for the primary purpose of developing West Virginia's

natural resources. Each sought instead to link the East with the rich agricultural lands and rapidly developing industrial cities of the Midwest. Accordingly, both quickly pushed their tracks westward into Ohio and beyond. In most areas it wasn't until investors began building feeder lines, branching out from the C&O and B&O into West Virginia's narrow and rugged valleys, that the coal riches were tapped.

Meanwhile, new through lines were laid out across southern West Virginia with the express purpose of providing access to the rich coal deposits there. Chief among these was the Norfolk & Western Railway. The

N&W entered West Virginia in 1883 and its Flat Top Mountain extension was built in 1884-86. The N&W reached the Ohio River at Kenova in 1892, crossed there and headed on to Portsmouth, Ohio, connecting to Cincinnati and Columbus.

The N&W — and the coal mining it spawned — transformed the remote mountain empire of southern West Virginia. In 1888, Bluefield was only a flag station on the farm of John B. Higginbotham. The next year it was incorporated as a town, with a population of about 600. By 1900, Bluefield had a population of 4,644 and by 1910, it had more than doubled to 11,188. The coal-fired growth

aug 1915

Bluefield grew up around the
Norfolk & Western train yard
(above), which still is an important
part of the city (left).

of other southern West Virginia towns — Princeton, Welch, Pineville, Madison, Logan and Williamson — was no less spectacular. In 1933, when the Williamson Chamber of Commerce decided it needed a headquarters building, it elected to build it out of coal — 65 tons of it. The decision seemed, if unusual, nevertheless appropriate. Without coal, there might never have been a Williamson.

The railroads not only hauled West Virginia's coal to market, they also brought in train loads of workers. Before the coal boom, the southern counties had been sparsely populated. Thus, mine operators were forced to recruit labor. They brought in white Americans from older coal regions (carefully screened in an effort to keep out union organizers), black Americans from the South, and European immigrants. The southern coal counties developed a richly diverse population representing the religions, languages and nationalities of much of the world

Some argue that the history of West Virginia from, say, 1880 to the 1950s, when mechanization began slashing mine employment, is the history of coal. Nowhere is that more true than in the state's southern counties — especially Boone, Logan, Mingo, Raleigh, Fayette, Wyoming and McDowell. It was

Robert C. Byrd

"Senator Byrd works 24 hours a day, seven days a week, 365 days a year helping the people of West Virginia. He is the champion of the interests of the people of West Virginia."

That's high praise, especially considering that it comes from the leader of the opposing party — U.S. Senate Majority Leader Robert C. Dole, a Kansas Republican. Dole's comment came on the Senate floor July 27, 1995, as the U.S. Senate honored Byrd for casting his 14,000th Senate vote. No senator has ever cast more votes. But then, setting political records is old hat for Byrd, one of only three senators ever to be elected to seven six-year terms.

Not bad for a poor boy from the southern coal country.

Robert Carlyle Byrd was born Cornelius Calvin Sale Jr. in North Carolina in 1917. His mother died in the 1918 influenza epidemic and, honoring his wife's dying wish, his father, a factory worker with four other children to rear, gave the baby boy to his sister, Vlurma Sale, and her husband, Titus Dalton Byrd. They renamed the boy and moved to West Virginia.

In Mercer County, the elder Byrd first went to work in the mines, then tried his hand at farming. Robert started school and, at an early age, discovered the joy of learning.

Times were tough. Each day after school, the senator recalls, he had to go from house to house, collecting food scraps from neighbors to feed the hogs he and his foster father raised. As he walked, a pail in each hand, the scraps would slop out and stain his jeans.

"I didn't smell very nice," he says.

But Byrd learned to play the violin in the orchestra at Mark Twain High School — and graduated first in his class.

Sophia, Senator Byrd's hometown.

Jobs were scarce in 1934 West Virginia and college out of the question. Byrd found work as a gas station attendant, but had to walk from his house to the station every morning, a distance of four miles that seemed even longer in winter.

"Some mornings I was lucky and got a ride on the bread truck," he recalls.

His foster mother took in lodgers and one loaned Byrd his overcoat and hat to wear. He had none of his own.

When he landed a job as produce boy at a coal company store, Byrd and his high school sweetheart, Erma, married. They set up housekeeping in two upstairs rooms of a company house.

Today, Byrd, leafing through old pay stubs, recalls there were weeks when his charges at the company store came to more than his meager pay.

After working his way through a meatcutter's manual at night, studying at the kitchen table, Byrd got a job as a butcher. Later, during World War II, he worked as a welder at shipyards in Baltimore and Tampa. Returning to West Virginia, he ran for — and won — a seat in the House of Delegates.

Now Byrd has held more legislative offices than anyone else in West Virginia history — serving in the House of Delegates, the state Senate, the U.S. House and the U.S. Senate. He has never lost an election.

In recent years, using his seniority and skill, Senator Byrd has managed to steer more than $1 billion in federal spending to West Virginia, and his name is prominently displayed on hospitals, university buildings, bridges, roads and more. His critics in Congress and elsewhere have denounced his efforts, labeling him the "Prince of Pork." Byrd simply shrugs off their criticisms and keeps on working for the state he loves.

You have to strip away the surface to figure out what makes some politicians tick, layer by layer, like peeling an onion. Not so with Bob Byrd. As those who know him well can testify, he is exactly what he seems.

When Byrd talks about his love for his family, his state, his country — and, of course, for the U.S. Senate, where he has served since 1958 — he means every word of it. When he talks about the virtues of hard work, faith in God, responsible citizenship and honesty, he means that. That's exactly the way he has lived his own life.

The term "living legend" is frequently overused. But it's the only way to describe Robert C. Byrd.

Labor history was made at the town of Matewan (above) in 1920, when Police Chief Sid Hatfield led miners against coal company gunmen.

A flood wall protects Williamson from the unpredictable Tug Fork.

even the appeals of famed union organizer Mother Jones could get the miners to turn around and go home. Eventually their ranks swelled to 10,000 or more.

Between the miners and Mingo County, however, was Logan County, where Sheriff Don Chafin, long in league with the coal companies, vowed to stop them. He organized an army of his own, made up of state police, deputies and mine guards, and the two sides clashed on the ridges of Blair Mountain. After four days of fighting the outcome was still inconclusive. But when President Warren G. Harding dispatched federal troops to the scene, the miners reluctantly surrendered, saying they could not fight against the flag many had served under in World War I.

Today, Matewan has turned back the clock. Money contributed by coal companies and the Benedum Foundation, among others, has helped restore what remains of Matewan to its 1920s appearance. Facades along the railroad tracks, which in 1920 formed the main street, have been restored and utility lines buried underground to keep the area looking as it did before electricity and telephones were commonplace. A recording, activated by a button installed on the wall of the old Matewan National Bank Building, tells the town's story, interspersed with comments from residents who

Welch, which boomed as a coalfields center early in the century (left), nestles among the mountains.

were children at the time.

The Matewan Massacre, all but forgotten over the years, was made familiar to millions when acclaimed film director John Sayles depicted it in his 1987 movie *Matewan*. Ironically, when Sayles came to West Virginia to film his movie, he couldn't do so in Matewan. The town's current preservation effort had yet to unfold, and the movie maker had to look elsewhere for the right setting because Matewan had changed so much over the years.

Sayles eventually took his cameras and cast to the nearly deserted New River ghost town of Thurmond, in Fayette County.

It was a good choice. During the first two decades of the 1900s, Thurmond was a classic coalfields boom town. With the huge amounts of coal brought in from area mines, it had the largest shipping revenues of any point on the Chesapeake & Ohio. Having many coal barons as patrons, Thurmond's banks were among the richest in the state. Fifteen passenger trains a day came through town and its busy C&O depot served nearly 100,000 travelers a year. The town's hotels and boarding houses were constantly full, while its stores — as well as its saloons and houses of ill repute — did a brisk business.

The railroad lay at the heart of Thurmond's prosperity and the coming of better highways undercut the town's advantage. The replacement of coal-fired steam locomotives with oil-burning diesels at mid-century hastened Thurmond's decline. Businesses closed and most residents moved on. By the time filmmaker Sayles arrived, Thurmond had exactly the ghost-town atmosphere he was looking for.

But today, the U.S. Park Service has breathed welcome new life into the long-deserted Thurmond depot, giving it a $2.5 million restoration to bring visitors face-to-face with the New River Gorge's rich history as a mining and railroading center.

The station's ticket office, dispatcher's office and yardmaster's offices have been restored to their original appearance, while the rest of the 125-foot long building houses interpretive displays, a book and gift shop, restrooms, Park Service offices and a waiting room for The Cardinal — the lone Amtrak train that still stops there. Outside, an overlook provides great views of whitewater raft traffic on the New River and a vintage-1880s bridge that carries a rail spur across the river to Southside Junction.

If the restored Thurmond station gives an idea of a colorful town life in the days when coal was king, a visit to the Beckley Exhibition Mine offers a re-

The Itmann company store is an outstanding example of surviving coalfields architecture.

The coal rush brought the peoples and religions of much of the world together in southern West Virginia.

minder of the dangerous, back-breaking work required of that era's miners.

Visitors ride a "man trip" car 1,500 feet underground into what, from 1890 to 1910, was an actual working mine. The miners worked a 30-inch coal seam, meaning that the miners labored on their hands and knees, often crawling as much as a quarter of a mile, holding their lunch bucket with their teeth, to get to the working coal face. In those days, miners worked by the ton, paid only for what they produced. And they labored in virtual darkness, with just flickering carbide helmet lights to see by. It was a hard way to make a living.

Near the entrance of the Exhibition Mine is a restored coal-camp house. Since most mines were opened in lightly settled areas, little housing was available for the vast influx of laborers. So the coal companies built their own towns. The mine opening, rail siding and tipple for loading the rail cars were situated first, then in the remaining space, whether it was a valley floor or steep hillside, the town was constructed.

The houses generally were rudimentary, with only three or four rooms and a privy out back. The typical coal camp might contain houses of only two or three different designs and sizes, painted all the same, with the

BuckHarless

He has been a coal miner and a sawmill operator, a bank executive and more. And, although his own formal education ended with high school, he has a fistful of honorary degrees from various institutions, including West Virginia University and Marshall.

He is James H. Harless of Gilbert, known to virtually one and all as "Buck."

Born in 1919 in Logan County, Harless was orphaned at an early age and went to live with an aunt in the little town of Gilbert in Mingo County.

"We were very poor," he recalls, "but I was given such an abundance of love. I saw her work with what few physical things she had, but with a genuine concern for other people. We always had a drunk eating with us, or some poor old codger who had no place to go. Our table was always crowded and we never had that much on the table. I think if I have any semblance of compassion, that's where I got it."

The future entrepreneur started his first business — selling scrap metal to a junk yard — at age 10. Not satisfied with just collecting on his own, he passed word to his buddies that he'd buy any scrap metal they could find. The budding enterprise came to a halt when parents began to notice serious shortages in their kitchen cupboards. "When the kids starting stealing their moms' pots and pans and selling them to me, I had to stop," he says.

Harless graduated from Gilbert High School. After a stint in the military, he returned to West Virginia and went to work as a miner.

In 1947, Harless took what he describes as a "sizable gamble" and quit his mining job to become part owner and manager of a sawmill. He later bought out his partners and expanded operations. In 1966, he sold his company, Gilbert Lumber Company, to Georgia Pacific Corporation. The shares of stock he received in the deal made him the largest private stockholder in that timber industry giant.

Under his contract with Georgia Pacific, Harless agreed not to operate a sawmill for 10 years. So he turned his business energies elsewhere, founding the Dash Coal Company. Later, Dash became the coal division of Gilbert Imported Hardwoods, a firm importing mahogany, teak, balsa and other woods. Along the way, Harless started sawmill operations in Brazil and Ecuador, the first U.S. operator to do so.

Harless has founded two banks — in Gilbert and Logan — and has been involved in various other business efforts over the years.

And he has shared the fruits of his success.

"Everything we have, or ever will have, we are stewards of,"

Buck Harless, Mingo County entrepreneur.

he says. "It is to be handled for the benefit of the most people possible. When you are lucky and successful, you feel an obligation."

Harless hasn't hesitated to put that philosophy into practice, aiding a long list of organizations and groups over the years. And no one — including his accountant — likely knows the number of individuals he has helped when they needed it.

He has been active in the Presbyterian Church, serving as an elder in his congregation, past moderator of the Presbytery of Greenbrier, and a director of the Greenbrier Mission Development Fund.

Even though Harless didn't go to college himself, he's been a particular friend to West Virginia higher education for more than 40 years. He has generously underwritten scholarships and provided other financial support for both WVU and Marshall University, and has served on the foundations and advisory boards of both.

"We talk about the problems of West Virginia," he says, "but one of the biggest is the failure of citizens to recognize the importance of higher education. If this state is ever going to take its place among its sister states, it is going to have to put more money into higher education."

Some individuals contribute their time. Some their money. Buck Harless shares both.

As Marshall President J. Wade Gilley has said: "Buck Harless could have chosen many years ago to reside in a fancy resort community, anywhere in the world. He could have forgotten the mountains from which he came, his many years of hard work, the people who labored beside him. That was not, and is not, Buck's way."

Tourists acquaint themselves with the underground world at Beckley Exhibition Mine.

Timbering skills are remembered at Twin Falls State Park.

smallest and cheapest reserved for blacks. More substantial houses were built for mine superintendents, usually located at a distance from those of the workers, and often on a hillside overlooking the town. A recent addition to the Beckley Exhibition Mine is a superintendent's house originally built in 1906 by coal baron Samuel Dixon for his Raleigh County mining town of Skelton, named after his birthplace in England. The old house was dismantled, moved to the grounds of the Exhibition Mine and there reassembled.

The typical coal camp had two churches and two schools — one of each for whites and blacks — and, of course, the company

store. Often the only retail outlet within reach of mining families, the company store stocked food, clothing, household furnishings, mine supplies and most anything else a miner or his family might need. Companies usually issued scrip, a form of currency negotiable only at their stores. Many exerted ruthless pressure on the miners to trade at their stores, frequently charging excessive prices. An enlightened few strived to provide good merchandise at fair prices.

Today, West Virginia's company towns and company stores are fading fast. Some small towns — Nellis in Boone County, Dehue and Holden in Logan, Coalwood in McDowell,

Chatteroy and Cinderella in Mingo — still reveal their coal-camp origins.

Excellent surviving examples of the company store can be found at Itmann in Wyoming County and Scarbro in Fayette County. Built in 1923 of cut stone by Isaac T. Mann's Pocahontas Fuel Company, the Itmann store was designed by Bluefield's Alex B. Mahood, one of the most important West Virginia architects of that day. The Scarbro store was built in 1900 by Justus Collins, owner of the Whipple Colliery and other mines. It is of unusual design, with a six-sided first floor and an eight-sided second floor. In 1905, the mine changed hands

and the store became New River Company Store No. 4, a part of Sam Dixon's empire. The mine closed in 1957, but the building remained a working general store until the late 1980s.

If the old company stores represent a bygone way of life in the southern coal counties, there's perhaps no better symbol of the region's future than Corridor G, a four-lane highway that's being counted on to boost economic opportunities in southern West Virginia.

When the last sections of the 81-mile road are finished in late 1996 or early 1997, Corridor G will link Charleston and Williamson. Already, 61 miles of the road — from Charleston to

Recreation (above and above right) has joined mining as a major industry in the historic coalfields.

Remnants of the coal towns remain throughout southern West Virginia. This is Powhatan, McDowell County.

Chapmanville — have been completed, and new businesses are beginning to spread south from Charleston along the corridor. And that kind of job creation is the mission of the state's corridor system, an undertaking devised by the Appalachian Regional Commission and pushed by West Virginia's Senator Robert C. Byrd.

"The architects of the corridor highway system recognized that the waters of economic prosperity flow along concrete rivers," says Byrd. "If we build roads, then the jobs, tourists, new industry and a better economy will all come."

Bird's-Eye View of Charleston, W. Va. 1854. From a Painting.

Antebellum Charleston was already a thriving community. The city is built where the Elk River joins the Kanawha.

Opposite Page - Charleston celebrates its river heritage at the annual Sternwheel Regatta.

The Capital City

CHAPTER 7

In 1788, Colonel George Clendenin headed a band of tough frontiersmen who marched into the Kanawha Valley from Camp Union, now Lewisburg. Clendenin and his men had been dispatched to establish a military outpost as part of Virginia's system of frontier defense against the region's Indians. Exciting things have been happening on the banks of the Kanawha ever since. Charleston, the city that sprang from that humble log fort is now the commercial, cultural and governmental center of West Virginia — and the hub of a metropolitan area with more than 200,000 people.

Charleston is the gleaming gold dome of the state capitol rising in the morning mists along the Kanawha River. It's the bustling Town Center Mall. It's Sunrise Museum and Alleycats baseball at Watt Powell Park. It's the paddlewheeler *P.A. Denny* and the Sternwheel Regatta, an annual 10-day tribute to the city's riverboat days. It's concerts by the West Virginia Symphony and family outings at Coonskin Park.

Interstates 64, 77 and 79 converge in Charleston — as if to confirm the vision of George Clendenin, a member of the Virginia legislature, that the Kanawha Valley would be an important gateway for travelers. It was that vision that prompted

Clendenin to buy more than 1,000 acres of wilderness at the mouth of the Elk River. On December 19, 1794, the legislature designated 40 acres of Clendenin's land as a town. He named the town Charlestown, in honor of his late father Charles. The new city's name was frequently confused with that of Charles Town in Jefferson County, so in 1818 it was shortened to Charleston.

In 1796, Clendenin, disappointed in the new city's slow growth, sold his property to Joseph Ruffner, who moved to the valley from Page County, Virginia. In 1800, Charleston had only 12 houses and perhaps 65 residents. But a decade or so

later, the War of 1812 brought a boom to the Kanawha Valley. The war halted the importation of salt from the British West Indies and created a demand for the valley's so-called "red salt" (discolored from iron impurities), used to cure meat.

As early as 1797, Elisha Brooks had leased some property from Ruffner and sunk shallow wells. The brine from the wells, once boiled, yielded small amounts of salt, which Brooks sold. Ruffner died in 1802 and it fell to two of his sons, David and Joseph, to achieve his dream of large-scale salt production. In 1808, they sank deeper wells and struck brine so rich that 200 gallons yielded a bushel of salt, a

The Ruffners prospered with the community, moving from a sturdy log house (above) to a mansion by the Kanawha. Holly Grove mansion (left) is now part of the capitol complex.

Craik-Patton House symbolizes 19th century Charleston.

sharp contrast to the 500 gallons required from the shallow wells.

The success of the Ruffners attracted imitators, who sank their own wells and built their own furnaces. By 1815, both sides of the Kanawha for about 10 miles above Charleston were lined with furnaces. Saltmaking spawned related industries: the construction of flatboats, the making of barrels and the mining of coal to fire the furnaces. And the salt industry also introduced a phenomenon that was to become a familiar problem in the valley over the years. As one contemporary observer wrote, "The furnaces send up columns of smoke and vapor which ... darken the atmosphere overhead and give the valley a gloomy appearance."

In 1815, another Ruffner son, Daniel, built Holly Grove mansion, a handsome, three-story brick structure. As was common for owners of large homes at the time, Ruffner made rooms and meals available for travelers. Among Holly Grove's famous guests: President Andrew Jackson, Henry Clay and John J. Audubon. Today, the old mansion still stands on Kanawha Boulevard, a working part of the capitol complex.

George Clendenin had given up on his city too soon. By 1825, steamboats connected Charleston with various points up and down the Ohio River.

21325—Kanawha Street, Looking West,
CHARLESTON, W. Va.

Charleston streets bustled even
before they knew rubber tires and
internal combustion.

Early in 1827, a once-a-week
stagecoach began operating over
the James River and Kanawha
Turnpike between Charleston
and Lewisburg. The one-way fare
was $7. By the early 1840s,
Charleston boasted nine lawyers,
four physicians, numerous
skilled tradesmen and several
dry goods merchants, grocery
stores and specialty shops.

The outbreak of the Civil
War on April 12, 1861, and the
secession of Virginia from the
Union five days later found
Charleston a town of divided
loyalties. Like most delegates
from Virginia's western counties,
Kanawha County's two represen-
tatives to the Virginia State
Convention voted against

secession, but the area had many
Southern sympathizers.

On June 26, 1861, a
Confederate force entered
Charleston without firing a shot.
A one-day battle at Scary Creek
in Putnam County on July 17
was a Confederate victory, but
the Confederates knew they
risked being encircled and
trapped in Charleston. On July
24, they retreated. The next day
Union troops moved into the city,
also without firing a shot. On
October 24, with Charleston still
under federal occupation, the
people of western Virginia voted
their approval to the formation
of a new state.

In the Spring of 1862, the
Charleston area was guarded by

Glenwood, the Quarrier family
mansion, has greeted many
springtimes on the city's west side.

The Kanawha River at Red House, downstream from Charleston.

General Hospital, Charleston, W. Va.

The old General Hospital, now demolished, is among the city's lost landmarks.

only a meager force when Confederate troops arrived on the south bank of the Kanawha, near the present University of Charleston, and began shelling the town. His fellow officers later questioned the wisdom of his decision, but Union General Joseph A.J. Lightburn ordered a retreat. Charleston was an important Union supply depot and Lightburn said he was fearful the Confederates would capture the city's vast stores. Loading what supplies they could on wagons, his men retreated toward Ripley. Before they left, they torched a half-dozen buildings containing the rest.

The Confederates chose not to pursue Lightburn but instead busied themselves seizing supplies of salt for shipment to Richmond, where salt was desperately needed. The day's fighting was only a footnote in Civil War history. Nonetheless, it cost the lives of 25 men on the Union side and 18 on the Confederate. The Southerners held the city for about six weeks, then retreated. Union troops staged a bloodless reoccupation and stayed until the war's end.

When West Virginia was admitted to the Union in 1863, Wheeling, then a metropolis of 14,083, was selected as the new state's capital. There was no indication that tiny Charleston, with its population of 1,520, would one day have that honor.

But in 1869 Charleston offered $50,000 to build a capitol if the state government was moved, and the Legislature approved the transfer. On March 20, 1870, the steamboat *Mountain Boy* arrived in Charleston, carrying Governor William E. Stevenson, other officials, and all the trappings of state government. A modest three-story structure was built and would be the state's seat of government until 1875. Then, in a stunning blow to the city, the Legislature voted to return the capitol to Wheeling. A court challenge of the move failed, but, in 1877, Charleston convinced the Legislature to put the issue of a permanent capital to a statewide public vote. Three cities were listed on the ballot: Martinsburg, Clarksburg and Charleston, which proved the runaway winner. It would be 1885, however, before state government actually returned to the banks of the Kanawha.

In 1873, the Chesapeake & Ohio Railway's tracks reached Charleston and soon feeder lines were built into the rich coal lands on Cabin Creek, Paint Creek and other Kanawha River tributaries. In 1875, only three Kanawha County mines shipped coal to outside markets. Eight years later, that number had grown to 47. The railroads, combined with the locks and dams constructed on the Kanawha, paved the way for

Kathy Mattea

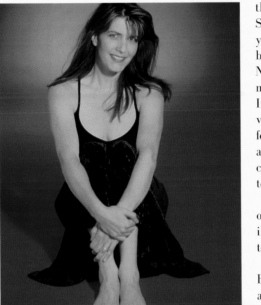

Music has been a part of Kathy Mattea's life for as long as she can remember. Growing up in the Cross Lanes area, just outside Charleston, she played guitar and sang throughout high school, then joined a bluegrass group called Pennsboro while at West Virginia University.

Today, she's one of the biggest stars in the world of country music.

Her road to stardom started when the leader of Pennsboro packed up for Nashville and Mattea decided to leave school to give it a try for herself. She wrote the song, "Leaving West Virginia" about her experience and, some years later, recorded it on one of her albums.

Today, she realizes what a big chance she was taking by walking away from her college studies.

"I was young and stupid, basically," she says. "My dad thought I would be back before the next semester. My parents' biggest fear was that I would fail and have no education to fall back on."

In Nashville, Mattea worked as a tour guide at the Country Music Hall of Fame. There she earned $90 a week for telling wide-eyed tourists about the instruments and costumes on display and the Elvis Presley Cadillac.

"There were times when you could see what a thrill it was for people," she recalls. "One day a 90-year-old man came up to me in tears. He said he'd listened to the Grand Ole Opry all his life, and he was going that night. This was the biggest moment of his life."

Mattea worked at other odd jobs, including a stint as a waitress, took voice lessons and eventually cut a demo tape that got her some studio work. Word of her talent spread and soon she was in demand as a backup singer behind other musical artists. She got her big break when record executives began asking who the singer was they were hearing so often. Polygram Records signed her to a contract in 1983.

Her debut album produced three hit singles. She was on her way. She toured extensively and in her first year as a single artist was hailed by both *Billboard* and *Cashbox* as "Top New Female Artist." More albums, more hits and more honors followed. In 1989 and again in 1990, she was voted the Country Music Association's female vocalist of the year. Her voice and face became a familiar part of TV commercials promoting West Virginia tourism.

A story Mattea tells about an outdoor concert in Florida aptly illustrates the magic bond she is able to establish with her audience.

She was singing "Where've You Been," her poignant hit about an aged, ailing married couple who are re-united in a hospital room. She came to the last chorus. "Suddenly," she recalls, "the loudspeaker booms out. 'Edith Thomas, come to the Swine Barn.' I'm standing there thinking, so what do I do now? Finish the song? Make some comment? I looked down at a woman crying her eyes out, and I realized she never heard the announcement because she was so into the lyrics. So I went ahead and finished."

Even though Mattea herself had doubts that "Where've You Been" could be a commercial hit, an army of record-buyers proved her wrong. The song won a Grammy — a dream come true for the West Virginia singer.

But Mattea's dream turned into a nightmare in 1992 when she learned that chronic throat blisters would require surgery. Although the condition was not life-threatening, doctors warned her that with or without surgery, she might never sing again.

Mattea recalls that at first she was angry. Then, after she found herself sharing a medical waiting room with cheerful patients battling deadly cancers, she gained a new perspective.

"I realized I'm one of the lucky ones. Life is the gift; singing is the secondary gift. No matter how this turns out, I am probably going to walk out of here and go on with my life whether I am a professional singer or not."

Happily for Mattea and her many fans, surgery cured her condition and exercise restored the strength to her voice.

Even so, she says her illness forever changed her outlook. It convinced her to save more time for family and friends and it reminded her of who she is and where she's from.

"My roots run deep," she says. "I think of myself as a West Virginian who happens to live in Tennessee."

West Virginia's capitol has a complex history, having moved twice from Wheeling to Charleston, and later from downtown Charleston to the city's east end. The red brick downtown capitol (above) burned in 1921, and a grand new building (below) was soon under construction. Today the state capitol (right) is among West Virginia's treasures.

Charleston's transformation from a sleepy little city into a bustling industrial and commercial center.

It was World War I that turned the Kanawha Valley into "Chemical Valley." Historian Otis K. Rice has noted that the war cut off America's supplies of German-made chemicals and necessitated the building of a munitions industry. "During the war the federal government itself laid the basis for the chemical industry in the Kanawha Valley by undertaking construction of a high-explosives plant at Nitro and a mustard gas plant at Belle. Other major chemical firms of the Kanawha Valley, including Union Carbide and Du Pont, had their origins in World War I or the years immediately following," Rice wrote.

Along with chemicals, glass became an important industry in the Kanawha Valley. In 1920, the Libbey-Owens-Ford Glass Company erected a large plant for making window glass, and nearby an affiliated company built a large bottle plant. Both plants, now closed, made use of inventions by Michael J. Owens, a native West Virginian, which made older glass-making methods obsolete.

By the 1920s, the old locks and dams on the Kanawha River were obsolete. Completion of the last of 50 new locks and dams on the Ohio River in 1929, giving it a nine-foot channel from Pittsburgh all the way to Cairo, Illinois, prompted demands for similar improvements on the Kanawha. In the 1920s, the U.S. Army Corps of Engineers replaced the 10 old dams on the Kanawha with three new roller-type dams located at Winfield, Marmet and London. Coal traffic on the Kanawha remained substantial but petroleum products, chemicals and other products accounted for an increasing share of river cargo.

Coal, chemicals and glass were the building blocks of Charleston's growth, but ask West Virginians who live outside the Kanawha Valley what they think of when you say "Charleston" and most will answer "state government." And certainly its role as the seat of government

Turnpike to Somewhere

From the first, the West Virginia turnpike was envisioned as a four-lane roadway stretching from Charleston south to Princeton. But the state's rugged terrain sent costs skyrocketing and forced a much-decried decision to construct an initial two lanes and add the other two later.

Nonetheless, the road that opened in 1954 was an engineering marvel. A highlight was the 2,600-foot Memorial Tunnel, which eliminated the need for the turnpike to go an additional 26 miles by existing routes. The $5 million tunnel was said to be the first in the nation to be equipped with closed-circuit TV cameras to monitor traffic. Immediately south of the tunnel was the Bender bridge, named for World War II hero Stanley Bender of Fayette County, a winner of the Congressional Medal of Honor. Motorists traveling south on the turnpike emerged from the tunnel to find themselves crossing a bridge that, at 282 feet, was the highest east of the Mississippi River.

Yet, despite the impressive engineering that went into it, the turnpike was initially an economic disaster. Traffic for the toll road fell far short of projections, primarily because it linked up with no other significant highways. *The Saturday Evening Post* called the highway a "Turnpike to Nowhere."

The coming of the interstate systems offered better connections and changed things dramatically. Soon the turnpike became a major north-south artery, carrying more and more cars and trucks each year. At the same time, it also chalked up a staggering toll of traffic deaths. Many motorists accustomed to driving four-lane interstates found the two-lane turnpike a difficult — and sometimes deadly — challenge.

WEST VIRGINIA STATE ARCHIVES

The West Virginia Turnpike was originally built as a two-lane toll road, with occasional three-lane passing zones. Traffic was sparse in the early days.

Expanding the turnpike to four lanes proved to be an even tougher and costlier proposition than building it. In 1987, when Governor Arch Moore presided over ceremonies marking the project's completion, he noted that "a whole generation of West Virginians ... cannot remember a time when the West Virginia Turnpike wasn't under construction." The upgrading of the turnpike to four lanes had taken 14 years and cost $683 million.

More than $35 million went to moving 10 million cubic yards of earth and building a giant "open cut" that now accommodates all four lanes of the turnpike, bypassing both the Memorial Tunnel and the Bender Bridge. The tunnel was closed and the bridge demolished.

Today, a new chapter in turnpike history is opening, as completion nears for Tamarack, a new arts and crafts center. Located adjacent to the Beckley Travel Plaza at Milepost 44, the center will offer a year-round program of performing arts and crafts workshops. In addition to the retail sales area, it will include a display gallery, theater, nature trails and a food court featuring West Virginia foods.

STEPHEN J. SHAULTA, JR.

WEST VIRGINIA STATE ARCHIVES

Interstate I-64 (above) sweeps across the Kanawha River into Charleston's modern downtown business district. Earlier in the century, the waterfront Union Building (left) ruled the city skyline.

has been a major factor in the city's growth and prosperity.

When state government returned to Charleston from Wheeling in 1885, it set up shop in a new red brick capitol, topped with a 194-foot clock tower. The building cost $389,923.58 to erect and occupied the downtown block bounded by Washington and Lee and Capitol and Dickinson streets. With the addition of an annex several years later at the corner of Hale and Lee streets, it adequately served the needs of state government of that day.

On the afternoon of January 3, 1921, plumes of smoke were seen rising from the top of the capitol. Soon thou-

sands of spectators, including Governor John J. Cornwell, who emerged from a side door, witnessed the destruction of the picturesque, vine-covered building. Viewers of the fire were treated to an unexpected display of fireworks, as thousands of rounds of ammunition exploded and fueled the raging flames. The ammunition had been confiscated as a result of recent unrest in the coalfields and stored in the capitol for safekeeping. Fortunately, many important state documents escaped destruction in the fire because they were stored in the annex.

Almost immediately, Governor Cornwell and other leaders determined that West

Virginia would construct a grand, new capitol that would be a permanent and enduring monument to statehood. In the meantime, state government moved into hastily-constructed temporary quarters. Built of wood and wallboard, it was dubbed the "Cardboard Capitol." Ironically it, too, would be destroyed by fire — on March 2, 1927.

The Legislature created a Capitol Building Commission, which, after scrutinizing the credentials of many of the country's leading architects, selected noted architect Cass Gilbert to design the new capitol. Gilbert designed the Woolworth Building in New York, capitol

buildings in Minnesota and Arkansas, and buildings on several college and university campuses. Rather than rebuilding at the old site, the commission decided the new capitol should be erected in the less congested eastern end of the city, where there would be ample room for future expansion. Designed by Gilbert in the Italian Renaissance style, the new capitol was built in stages. The west wing was finished first, in 1925, and the east wing in 1927. The building's central portion, with its soaring dome, was dedicated on June 20, 1932, the state's 69th birthday.

The new capitol cost $10 million, and many thought

The chemical industry provides employment for many residents of Charleston and the Kanawha Valley.

The P.A. Denny

The *P.A. Denny* is a familiar sight at the Charleston riverfront, but few know the sternwheeler's remarkable story.

In 1870, Charles Ward emigrated to the United States from his native England. He lived briefly in Cincinnati, then moved to Charleston to assist in the installation of the Kanawha Valley's first gas plant.

In 1872, Ward started his own business and in 1878 built a boiler for the boat *Wild*

The "P.A. Denny" was born on the Kanawha River, and is perfecty at home there.

Goose. The packet *Katydid* was fitted with the second boiler that Ward made. She originally ran between Charleston and Gallipolis, Ohio. Known for her swiftness, the *Katydid* rushed the Cincinnati papers to Charleston on the day of issue.

The Charles Ward Engineering Works eventually built a wide variety of boats with Ward-built boilers which were considered the world's best by many marine designers. In World War I, the Navy ordered 400 of them.

In 1930, shortly before the Great Depression forced it out of business, Ward Engineering built the towboat *Scott*, used by the Louisville District of the U.S. Army Corps of Engineers until 1954.

Charleston riverman Pete Denny bought the *Scott* in 1973, carefully rebuilt her from the hull up, and renamed her the *Robin D. Too.* The spunky riverboat earned the reputation of being one of the fastest sternwheelers of her size on the river when Denny piloted her to a surprise victory in a 1974 race staged for that year's Sternwheel Regatta. Denny's death in 1975 prompted long-time friend Lawson Hamilton to purchase the riverboat and rename her in honor of her former pilot.

Unlike many excursion boats that have fake paddlewheels strictly for show, the 200-passenger *P.A. Denny*, now operated by the Charleston Festival Commission, is the real thing — an authentic sternwheeler powered up and down the river by its big splashing paddlewheel.

TODD A. HANSON

STEPHEN J. SHALUTA, JR.

The Sternwheel Regatta is the biggest event on Charleston's calendar. The riverfront overflows with boats, crowds and lots of good music.

it outrageous for the state to lavish that kind of money on a monumental building at a time when West Virginians, like other Americans, were coping with the ravages of the Great Depression. But the money proved a wise investment. The majestic structure has served the state well and each year attracts thousands of admiring visitors.

In 1940, on the eve of World War II, when America

again would turn to the Kanawha Valley for the chemicals and munitions it needed. Charleston constructed the Kanawha Boulevard, a four-lane roadway along the north bank of the Kanawha from the Patrick Street Bridge to the city's East End. Its construction required the demolition of several buildings and the restructuring of the river bank, but it gave Charleston not only an efficient traffic artery

but also a handsome new riverfront that became one of its greatest assets.

Another important transportation link was forged in 1947, with the construction of Kanawha Airport on top of Coonskin Ridge, overlooking the city.

The coming of the Interstate highway system in the late 1960s saw Charlestonians bitterly divided as to where their new super-highways should be routed. The initial plan was to bring the new roads straight into the downtown, but many people insisted the roads should skirt the city, thus avoiding the forced relocation of homes and businesses. Eventually, the matter ended up in court. The final

decision: the roads were routed downtown. Today, Interstates 64, 77 and 79 converge in Charleston and, as a result, virtually every section of West Virginia, other than the Eastern Panhandle, is no more than a few hours away from Charleston by car.

In 1976, a $14 million Cultural Center opened its doors as part of the Capitol Complex. The Cultural Center is a colorful showcase for state artists as well as the state's history and heritage. Visitors enjoy a variety of permanent and changing exhibits and collections. The center's theater is home to West Virginia Public Radio's *Mountain Stage*, a weekly two-hour musical show that's broadcast on 127 radio

The Cultural Center hosts the nationally broadcast "Mountain Stage" radio show (left), the annual Vandalia Gathering folk festival (bottom), and other events.

Sunrise Science

Did you ever make giant soap bubbles? Weave a web of lightning from your finger tips? Suspend a beach ball on a column of air? Bend light? Create a rainbow?

Interactive exhibits at Sunrise Museum's Science Hall enable young visitors (along with moms and dads, too) to try their hands at these and other imaginative tasks, all designed to provide a fun-filled introduction to the world of science.

Perched above the Kanawha River overlooking Charleston, Sunrise Museum is housed in two historic mansions built by William A. MacCorkle, who served as West Virginia governor from 1893 to 1897. One of the two houses an art gallery, the other a science hall, including — until recently — a collection of small animals in a basement zoo.

Long-range plans for Sunrise call for its move to a new building envisioned for Charleston's expanding downtown. But the museum's board of directors decided not to wait until then to under-take major changes, including a new mission for the museum — art, science and technology.

Study after study has shown that American children lag far behind youngsters in other countries when it comes to science and math. The Sunrise board had those studies very much in mind when charting a new path for the children's museum.

New homes were found for the animals in the basement zoo, and the museum's dusty hodgepodge of history and nature exhibits cleared away to make way for the new hands-on exhibits that have made what's now called Sunrise Science Hall a magnet for school tours from West Virginia and adjoining states.

Downtown Charleston is graced by the newly built Haddad Riverfront Park.

Charleston's retail hub is Town Center Mall, located in the heart of the city.

stations around the nation. Hosted by popular singer-songwriter Larry Groce, the show offers many kinds of music, from alternative to zydeco. Musical artists appearing on the show range from relative unknowns to such stars as Joan Baez, Judy Collins, Lyle Lovett, Mary Chapin-Carpenter and, of course, West Virginia native Kathy Mattea. When the rock group R.E.M. released its "Out of Time" album, it made only three broadcast appearances — on *Saturday Night Live*, on MTV's *Unplugged* and *Mountain Stage*.

Music is also the big drawing card at Charleston's annual Sternwheel Regatta. Since starting out in 1970 as a modest celebration of the city's river heritage, the regatta has mushroomed into a yearly event that features some of the biggest names in pop music and attracts thousands of fun-seekers to the river. Today, the regatta is located at the city's handsome new $8 million Haddad Riverfront Park, named for Charleston businessman Fred Haddad who helped finance its construction.

In 1983, the Charleston Town Center, a modern three-story downtown mall, opened for business. The competition from the new mall proved too much for many long-time Charleston retailers, who were forced to close their doors. But former

STEPHEN J. SHALUTA, JR.

The city as twilight falls, during the Sternwheel Regatta.

Capitol Street has been restored to its historic charm.

©STEVE PAYNE

mayor John Hutchinson speaks for many when he describes the Town Center as pivotal to the city's future: "While other cities ... have seen their tax base destroyed by interstates and other highway systems that encouraged urban sprawl, Charleston's successful location of our primary shopping complex in our downtown area has guaranteed for decades a strong and healthy retail center and a viable and expanding tax base."

Today, Charleston and the Kanawha Valley bear scant resemblance to the wilderness that greeted George Clendenin and the valley's other early settlers. The salt wells that gave birth to the first economic boom along the Kanawha long since have ceased pumping. Wooded hillsides have given way to suburban communities that are home to thousands who work in the valley's many offices and plants, shop in its stores and enjoy its broad range of entertainment activities.

With the gold dome of the state Capitol gleaming in the sunlight by day and illuminated with spotlights at night, Charleston is very much at the center of West Virginia politics and government. But, more than that, it's the vibrant commercial and cultural hub of West Virginia. Clendenin's vision has been fulfilled beyond his wildest dreams.

Postcard view of Lewisburg, one of the historic communities on the Midland Trail.

Opposite Page - The New River Gorge offers breath-taking rock climbing.

Midland Trail and NewRiver

CHAPTER 8

H. O. Via, one of Huntington's early business leaders, arrived in the city as a young man in 1872, only a few months after it was chartered by the West Virginia Legislature. He had bounced his way from White Sulphur to Charleston on a far-from-comfortable stagecoach and then continued on to Huntington aboard a train, traveling over the newly laid tracks of the Chesapeake & Ohio Railway.

It took Via three days and nights to cover the 125 miles from White Sulphur Springs to Charleston. A half century later, in the 1920s, he recalled his trip: "It was not like riding one

of the modern buses.... Going up one mountain all the male passengers had to get out and walk. The mud was too deep and the hill too steep for the six horses pulling us. There were six of us men and one woman. The woman rode."

Via's route was the best available. For years the road from White Sulphur Springs westward was the only way of getting across the mountains to the Kanawha Valley and from there to the Ohio Valley. Tradition has it the path was first worn by herds of roaming buffalo and, later, by bands of Indians. First authorized in 1790 as the State Road by the Virginia General Assembly, it was developed as the

James River and Kanawha Turnpike and eventually became best known as the Midland Trail. With the coming of paved roads, it became U.S. Route 60.

Today, most motorists prefer the far quicker Interstate. But those travelers who are willing to take their time and drive the two-lane blacktop of U.S. 60 can get a glimpse into history that's denied those who hurry along the superhighway. The Midland Trail Scenic Highway Association works hard at luring tourists and others to the old road between Charleston and White Sulphur Springs. As a leaflet published by the association notes: "Generations of ghosts haunt every mile."

If you look closely, for instance, you might glimpse the ghost of Mary Draper Ingles. Captured by Indians, she escaped and made her 1755 return to civilization only after incredible hardship. On her return, she told about learning from her captors to make salt in the Kanawha Valley. This was good news to the Colonial Virginians, who were paying dearly for imported salt. Within decades, enterprising settlers were sinking salt wells. And by the early 1800s, Kanawha Salines — later to become the town of Malden — boasted more than two dozen wells. Demand for salt was a powerful incentive to build and maintain the

▲ GERALD S. RATLIFF ▼

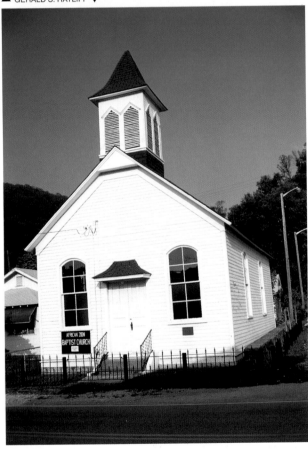

WEST VIRGINIA STATE ARCHIVES

The Old Stone House at Belle (above) is one of the oldest surviving structures along the Midland Trail.

Booker T. Washington was among the figures to shape Kanawha Valley history. His church was the African Zion Baptist Church (left) which still stands at Malden.

Midland Trail.

After the Civil War, a young boy newly freed from slavery traveled the road to Malden to work at the salt wells. The wife of a well owner recognized his intelligence and taught him to read. Booker T. Washington went on to found Tuskegee Institute and became a powerful spokesman for America's black citizens. A park honoring him stands on the site of his sister's home, where he once lived and often visited.

Today, Malden also is home to Cabin Creek Quilts, a cooperative that got its start in 1970 when Massachusetts-born James Thibeault, then a 21-year-old VISTA worker, gathered up

Pioneers black and white, slave and free, are buried at Virginia's Chapel, Cedar Grove.

The upper Kanawha was a working river in times past, as it is today.

West Virginia wintertime.

some quilts made by women who lived in the Cabin Creek area, loaded them in his beat-up Volkswagen and took them to a store on Cape Cod. "We sent out some notes to people and they came in," Thibeault recalls. "One of those first customers was Jackie Kennedy Onassis, who bought two and ordered two more." Thanks to the publicity resulting from the former first lady's purchase, Cabin Creek Quilts quickly found a wide demand for its handsome handiwork. In 1991 the co-op moved from rural Cabin Creek to Malden, where it bought and restored an old house for use as its first-ever retail outlet.

East of Malden on U.S. 60

are towns like Belle, Boomer, London and Alloy, home to some of the giant plants that have made the words "Kanawha Valley" synonymous with industry. At Belle, visitors are welcome at salt driller Samuel Shrewsbury's home. Built in 1810, the sandstone-block house stands as the last vestige of an 18th century farmstead engulfed by the chemical-plant town.

The town of Gauley Bridge hugs a steep corner of the mountain above the juncture of the New and Gauley rivers, the pivotal point between the New River Gorge and the Kanawha Valley. A fellow named Miller operated a ferry and tavern here until a toll bridge was built on

STEPHEN J. SHALUTA, JR.

The London Locks and Dam complex allows navigation on the upper section of the Kanawha River.

DAVID E. FATTALEH

Glen Ferris Inn has welcomed travelers since stagecoach days on the Midland Trail.

the new Kanawha Turnpike in 1822. The bridge stood until 1826, when a fire attributed to "persons interested in the ferry" destroyed it. A second bridge was built in 1848 — and burned by the retreating Confederate Army in 1861. Surviving stonework can still be seen.

Downstream, the river roars over a jagged ledge, forming picturesque Kanawha Falls. The nearby Glen Ferris Inn dates to 1839 when, as Stockton's Inn, it first offered hospitality to visiting stagecoaches, allowing weary riders to rest along the scenic falls. Today the Federal-style mansion, painstakingly restored in 1991, boasts 15 guest rooms and a fine dining room.

From the rugged mountaintop at Hawks Nest you may get a glimpse of not only the boulder-strewn New River far below but also, if you're lucky, the ghost of Mad Anne Bailey. Legend has it that when Indians besieged Fort Lee — now Charleston — in 1788, Mad Anne set off for help and, to confound her pursuers, rode her horse off Hawks Nest cliff, thus saving the day — and her scalp.

There are other ghosts, as well. In the 1930s, the Hawks Nest Tunnel was punched through Gauley Mountain to divert part of the waters of the New River to a hydroelectric generating station. This was the Great Depression. Hundreds of

Mary Lee Settle

Novelist Mary Lee Settle says she never really intended to be a writer. In fact, when a teacher at Sweet Briar College recognized her talent and urged her to set her sights on a writing career, she shrugged him off. "I tried to escape the effects of this suggestion," she says, "but did not succeed."

Had she done so, readers would have been deprived of some of the finest books ever written about West Virginia.

Settle was born in Charleston on July 29, 1918, and grew up chiefly in her mother's family home in nearby Cedar Grove, and in Greenbrier County and in Kentucky. She graduated from Charleston High School in 1936. She left Sweet Briar without a degree and in 1942 traveled to England, where she joined the Women's Auxiliary Air Force, an experience she later would describe in a memoir, *All the Brave Promises*.

After the war she remained in England, living there for 14 years. At first, she worked as a journalist and wrote a half-dozen plays that went unproduced. "The trouble with plays," she says, "is that you keep getting taken to lunch by people who say, 'Darling, it's a work of genius,' then you never hear from them again. I wrote my first novel because I decided that was the only way I could do the whole thing myself — be my own actors, set designer, producer, everything."

Settle's first novel, *The Love Eaters*, published in 1954, was set in an Appalachian coal town and hinged on the arrival of a crippled and embittered professional director, hired to train the local amateur theater group. It and a second novel were well received by the critics.

O Beulah Land, the first of five novels chronicling the settlement and development of West Virginia, was the result of three years of research at the British Museum. More years of research followed for the quintet's other volumes. "I knew when I began that it would be more than one book," Settle notes, "but I didn't expect it to keep me busy for 25 years."

O Beulah Land, the first of the five, centers around Virginian Jonathan Lacey, who scouts and surveys far into the mountains. He leads a group of settlers to claim and clear land he is given as a bounty. It is on this land, called Beulah by the group's preacher, that Lacey proves his strength. Subsequent volumes in the series trace the story both backwards, to 17th-Century England, and forward, to our own time.

O Beulah Land was praised by both the critics and the reading public. Despite good sales, however, getting the other four volumes published was not easy for Settle. In a 1988 article, she complained that over the many years it took her to complete the Quintet, the series had eight different publishers — four in hardback and another four in paper. "There have been only a few

©ANN BEATTIE

months when all five volumes were in print at the same time."

And is there, in the five volumes, a key scene? Yes, she says, and it's "the discovery of coal in West Virginia. That changed the entire lives of everyone living there; it became a feudal coal culture, as it were."

In addition to the Beulah Quintet, Settle has written a number of other books, both fiction and non-fiction. In 1978, she won the National Book Award for *Blood Tie*, a novel about a group of expatriates living in Turkey. *Choices*, her 13th novel, was published in 1995. In recent years, she has lived in Charleston and Norfolk and now makes her home in Charlottesville, Virginia.

"My view of life," she says, "has been helped by the fact that I have lived in places and with people who were dirt poor. Growing up in the coal country of West Virginia, I saw real poverty. Hemingway's view of grace under pressure had to do with going out and becoming a world correspondent or hunting big game. But to see real grace you just have to look next door to see what happens when illness or poverty hits."

Hawks Nest Lake impounds a stretch of New River (left), but the stream runs wild and free (above) in other parts of its gorge.

The New River Gorge is train country. This steam locomotive was photographed during an excursion run.

men desperate for jobs, many of them blacks from the South, signed on for the project. Even though the rock the tunnel was drilled through was 99 percent silica, few safety precautions were taken and many of the workers died from breathing tiny particles of silica. The tunnel is a great engineering achievement achieved at a frightful human cost.

Today, Hawks Nest State Park is one of the state's best-known tourist spots. A 31-room lodge sits 600 feet above the New River and has a restaurant, a coffee shop — and an awesome view of the gorge below. The park offers lots to do — an aerial tramway, self-guided paddle boat

and row boat tours on the New River, jet boat trips to the New River Gorge Bridge, hiking trails, picnic areas and a small museum of local history.

At nearby Winona is the Garvey House, built in 1916 as a coal-mine superintendent's residence. Now it is a bed and breakfast and a good headquarters for exploring the New River Gorge.

Despite its name, the New River actually is one of North America's oldest. It's roughly 65 million years old — give or take a few million. The New once was a much longer stream that geologists call the Teays, which flowed on through central Ohio, then Indiana and Illinois, emptying

Man vs. Machine

STEPHEN J. SHALUTA, JR.

"John Henry he could hammer,
"He could whistle, he could sing,
"Went to the mountain, early in the morning,
"Just to hear his hammer ring, Lawd, Lawd,
"Just to hear his hammer ring!"

John Henry, memorialized today in a Summers County statue and in the hearts of West Virginians, helped to build the Big Bend Tunnel.

Between 1871 and 1873, a work force of a thousand men and boys, many of them ex-slaves, bored a 6,500-foot railroad tunnel through the red shale of Big Bend Mountain between Hinton and Talcott in southern West Virginia.

That much is undisputed fact.

But legend and folk song tell us that one of those construction workers was a big and exceptionally strong ex-slave by the name of John Henry.

As a "steel driver," John Henry used a heavy hammer to drive a steel drill into the rock face. The drill was held by another worker called a "shaker." The shaker had to have steady nerves to hold the drill in place while the driver swung down his heavy hammer, only inches from his head and hands. A mistake could mean a crushed skull or mangled limb.

STEPHEN J. SHALUTA, JR.

Once large enough, the hole would accommodate an explosive charge that would blast the rock loose. After the fractured stone was gathered up and hauled away, the two-man crew would start its rhythmic hammering again.

One day, the legend says, a salesman showed up at the mountain with a new steam-powered drill he was anxious to sell to the company drilling the tunnel. John Henry and his fellow workers were unimpressed, and he boasted that he could drill a hole faster and deeper than the new-fangled invention.

The steam drill chugged away and did its best but it was no match for John Henry and his ringing hammer, who easily won the contest. But it would be the last hole that John Henry would drill. Exhausted, he made his way back to his cabin, lay down and "died with his hammer in his hand." He literally had worked himself to death.

Was John Henry a real person? Maybe so. Maybe not. There are no records to say. But, fact or fiction, his story lives on in one of the world's great folk tales.

"The people took John Henry to the White House,
"And they buried him in the sand,
"Every locomotive comes rolling by says,
"There lies a steel-driving man, Lawd, Lawd,
"There lies a steel-driving man!"

The New River Gorge bridge (above) is one of West Virginia's best known landmarks.

The rusting coal tipple at Nuttallburg is typical of earlier engineering in the gorge.

into the Mississippi. The last advance of glacial ice, about 10,000 years ago, buried most of the Teays and gouged out two new rivers in its place — the Kanawha and the Ohio.

The New River Gorge remained largely inaccessible until the coming of the railroad in 1873. The tracks of the Chesapeake & Ohio followed the riverbank and made possible the shipment of New River coal to the outside world. Towns grew up, briefly flourished, then were abandoned once the mines played out. In the southern or upstream stretches of the gorge, where the river is deceptively quiet with a broad flood plain, farming developed.

Today, 53 miles of the river and its gorge and another 40 miles of its tributaries are preserved as the New River Gorge National River, Gauley River National Recreation Area and Bluestone National Scenic River, all units of the National Park System.

A good place to begin a visit is the Park Service's Canyon Rim Visitors Center, on the north side of the river. Open year round, Canyon Rim provides a spectacular view of the gorge and the amazing U.S. Route 19 bridge. Trying to span the gorge with a highway was considered sheer folly until the late 1970s brought completion of the longest steel arch bridge in the

The New River is among the country's busiest whitewater rafting streams.

The gorge is haunted by the ghostly remains of more populous times. This chimney stands at a Fayette County coal town.

world. Each year, on the third Saturday in October, two lanes of the four-lane span are closed for Bridge Day. Parachute jumpers come from all over the country to leap over the edge of the bridge to the riverbed — 876 feet below. Thousands of people enjoy the entertainment, along with the many craft and food booths that line the length of the bridge for this single day each year.

Near the Canyon Rim Visitors Center is the Kaymoor Mine Trail, where you can walk several miles through the wilds of the gorge to the old Kaymoor Tipple, a reminder of the gorge's colorful mining past.

The New River drops 750 feet in the 50 miles from Bluestone Dam to Gauley Bridge, creating one of the finest whitewater rivers in the eastern United States. (By comparison, the slow-moving Mississippi falls 1,428 feet from Minnesota to the Gulf of Mexico, a distance of 2,300 miles.) In the southern end of the gorge, the New River is relatively placid. But north of Thurmond, the whitewater begins in earnest, with some rapids so difficult they should be attempted only by experienced and well-equipped adventurers.

The West Virginia Division of Tourism reports that whitewater rafting on the New and Gauley rivers is booming, growing 45 percent from 1990 to 1994.

But let's leave the New

The New River has its quieter stretches, perfect for boat fishing.

The picturesque mill at Babcock State Park is among the most photographed sites in West Virginia.

River Gorge behind and return our attention to our trip along U.S. 60. There a familiar spot for travelers over the years was the town of Ansted, which traces its roots to a group of Baptists who arrived in 1790 and originally called their little community New Hope. In 1861, its named was changed to honor David T. Ansted, a British coal speculator who had purchased much of the nearby land. Shortly after the Civil War, Confederate General George Imboden settled here to develop the region's coal resources. Julia Neale Jackson, the mother of General Thomas "Stonewall" Jackson, is buried in Ansted's Westlake Cemetery.

On the northeast rim of the New River Gorge, near Clifftop, is Babcock State Park, where a fast-running trout stream cascades down the mountain to turn the reconstructed Glade Creek grist mill. The park offers 26 vintage-1930 cabins, 50 campsites, a lake, pool and stables.

Also at Clifftop is Camp Washington-Carver, built in the days of segregation as West Virginia's black state 4-H camp. Dedicated in 1942, the camp complex is an unusually well-preserved example of a large-scale Works Progress Administration (WPA) project. Today, it's operated by the state Division of Culture and History and each summer offers a variety of events

Outdoor dramas at Grandview Amphitheater commemorate West Virginia's colorful heritage. This scene is from "Hatfields and McCoys."

The Mystery Hole

It's hard to miss the Mystery Hole as you drive along U.S. 60, just west of Hawks Nest State Park. It's the tin building with the Volkswagen Beetle hanging from its side.

For a dollar per person, owner Donald Wilson gives visitors a 10-minute tour of his roadside attraction.

It's an experience that's hard to describe. Most folks lose their sense of balance and many report that their head swims. You may feel as if you've been turned upside down. Nothing seems the way it ought to be. The usual laws of Nature — things like the law of gravity — don't seem to apply to the Mystery Hole.

Visitors generally leave with bewildered looks on their faces. Some say their visit was as close to the Twilight Zone as they care to get.

People from all walks of life have tried their hand at explaining the reasons behind the strange phenomena that occur at the Mystery Hole. Wilson just smiles — and welcomes the next group of paying customers.

Robert E. Lee's early Civil War service took place along the Midland Trail.

and activities.

Next, U.S. 60 curves its way across Sewell Mountain, known to Civil War buffs as the site of Lee's Trace, Confederate General Robert E. Lee's 1861 camp, where he first saw the Greenbrier County colt he would call Traveler. At the foot of the mountain is Rainelle. Founded as a sprawling lumber town, Rainelle took its name from John and W.T. Raine who owned the town — and what was once the world's largest hardwood mill.

Lewisburg was the unofficial western capital of Colonial Virginia and still boasts many historic 18th and 19th Century buildings.

Two early settlements here

The Mystery Hole is a familiar landmark and quirky favorite of motorists on the Midland Trail.

Winter is no stranger to West Virginia's southern mountains. The Lillydale covered bridge crosses a tributary of New River.

Lewisburg has the historic Old Stone Church (above) and its own Carnegie Hall.

— the first founded in 1751 — were destroyed by Indians. In 1770, a new fortified settlement was erected. It was from here, in 1774, that General Andrew Lewis led his expedition against Chief Cornstalk and his warriors. Cornstalk's defeat in the Battle of Point Pleasant brought an end to Indian raids in the Greenbrier Valley, thus allowing the settlement to grow. And the grateful citizens re-christened the place Lewisburg in the general's honor.

Lewisburg lures visitors with a wide variety of antique and specialty shops. Significantly, this is not a rebuilt, restored town. It's a town that's made up of buildings and homes that have been loved, cherished

The Greenbrier is among the world's foremost resorts. Its roots reach back to antebellum times in White Sulphur Springs.

Mountain bikers picnic on a trailside boulder.

and carefully maintained for generations. Many still are in the hands of the original families. In Lewisburg, there's history around virtually every corner.

The Old Stone Church, built in 1796, is said to be the oldest church building in continuous use west of the Alleghenies. Colonel John Stuart and his wife, Agatha, gave the land for the church site. Since the congregation numbered only 20 people, some of the women had to pitch in and help with the church's construction. Tradition maintains that women carried sand for the mortar by horseback from the Greenbrier River.

The General Lewis Inn, the oldest part of which dates back to 1834, still welcomes overnight guests. Its rooms are furnished with antiques and collectibles, but each also offers a TV and a private bath. And the inn's old-fashioned, home-cooked meals are a special treat.

Lewisburg's own Carnegie Hall, a 1902 gift to the town from steel tycoon Andrew Carnegie, has seen performers ranging from Isaac Stern to the band Asleep at the Wheel.

Lewisburg is the center of a thriving farming district which each August hosts the West Virginia State Fair. What began as a local fair for Greenbrier Countians in 1921 has grown into one of the nation's best known and most popular state fairs. Whatever your fancy — be it quilting or country music, harness racing or pedigreed livestock, carnival thrill rides or prize petunias — you'll find it at the West Virginia State Fair.

Just east of Lewisburg is White Sulphur Springs, named by the earliest settlers for the sulphur springs of clear transparency found on the grounds of what is now the Greenbrier Hotel, one of the world's finest resorts. But White Sulphur Springs is also the southern base for hikers who come to walk the Allegheny Trail — just as many of those early travelers walked the old Midland Trail on their way west.

GERALD S. RATLIFF

The South Branch Valley, as viewed from North Fork Mountain, typifies the beauty of the Potomac Highlands.

Opposite Page - Randolph County farm scene.

The Mountains and the Forest

CHAPTER 9

Larger than Rhode Island, West Virginia's lush Monongahela National Forest is one of the biggest patches of green to be found on the map of the eastern United States. Covering more than 900,000 acres, it dominates the state's Potomac Highlands, and stretches from Preston County in the north to Greenbrier County in the south.

Begun in 1915 with the purchase of a modest 7,200 acres, the Monongahela officially became a national forest in 1920. Much of the land Uncle Sam acquired for the forest had been cut over as part of the region's timbering boom during the 1890s and early 1900s. Some of

it was little more than bare hillsides, devoid of vegetation. Thousands of new trees were planted, and fire towers were erected to detect and prevent fires. In the 1930s, the Civilian Conservation Corps and the Works Progress Administration were active throughout West Virginia. Here in the forest they built access roads, sturdy stone and timber pavilions and other rustic structures, many of them still in use today.

Time and careful reforestation have revived the forest and given it a handsome new cover of trees. Its moist western side contains northern hardwoods such as cherry and maple, mixed with oak on the drier ridges and

yellow poplar in the valleys. The drier eastern side contains oak, cedar and — believe it or not — the occasional cactus. The forest is home to the headwaters of five major river systems and hundreds of miles of smaller streams.

The Monongahela is located within a day's drive of much of the East Coast and attracts more than two million visitors a year, making it one of West Virginia's premier tourist attractions. But it remains secluded and quiet, with ample opportunities for the visitor to escape crowds. The forest boasts some paved roads but many more are gravel. Restaurants, motels and service stations are few and far between. For those who really

want to get away from it all, the forest includes more than 120 square miles that have been designated as "wilderness areas." The term means exactly what it says — no roads, no structures, no logging, no motorized vehicles of any sort. The number of hikers in a group is limited to 10 to minimize human impact on the area.

Popular scenic spots in the forest include Dolly Sods, Cranberry Glades, Spruce Knob and Seneca Rocks.

The Dolly Sods Scenic Area derives its unusual name from a German family (Dahle) who grazed cattle on the grasslands (sods) in the 1800s. Its 10,000 acres include bogs.

A fly fisherman tries his luck in the waters of Shavers Fork.

The hardwoods of the Monongahela National Forest flame into color early each fall.

beaver ponds, clear mountain streams and 25 miles of hiking trails. Visitors can drive through the Scenic Area, but if you want to visit the adjacent Dolly Sods Wilderness, you will have to do so on foot or horseback.

In the Dolly Sods Wilderness, you will find steep canyons, sphagnum bogs, heath barrens, rhododendron thickets, forested mountainsides and spectacular rock outcroppings. You may also find, if you're not careful, a live mortar shell. During World War II, the Dolly Sods area was used for military exercises and live shells still occasionally turn up.

The Cranberry Glades Botanical Area has been likened to the tundra country of Alaska and northern Canada and is home to plant and animal life much like that found there. Don't expect polar bears or reindeer, but you will find teaberries and reindeer moss. A visitor center features informative exhibits and an audiovisual presentation. Years ago, wooden walkways were built to provide safe, dry footing for visitors to the area. Recently the walkways were widened and railings added to make them accessible to wheelchairs. The nearby Cranberry Wilderness includes 35,000 acres ideal for hiking, backpacking, hunting and fishing. As at the Dolly Sods Wilderness, all wheeled vehicles are prohibited.

At 4,861 feet, Spruce Knob is the highest point in West Virginia. At the top there's a grassy meadow, some wind-tortured trees and an observation tower for those willing to climb still higher. The commanding view from the tower is worth the effort. A lake stocked with trout attracts fishermen, especially in spring and fall, and in winter the mountain is popular with cross-country skiers.

You don't have to be a rock climber to be awed by the 900-foot tall strata of Tuscarora sandstone known as Seneca Rocks. Acclaimed for their striking beauty, Seneca Rocks, like the cliffs along the New River, attracts veteran rock climbers from all over the country. A hiking trail carries non-climbers safely to the top of the rocks, overlooking the valley below. A visitor center at the base was wiped out by the 1985 flood. It was rebuilt but then destroyed in a 1992 fire, thought to be arson. Now, connecting modular trailers are being used as a makeshift center, while work progresses on a new one.

Before the coming of white settlers, Native Americans knew Seneca Rocks well. An archaeological survey undertaken in connection with construction of the new visitor center unearthed arrowheads and other evidence suggesting there was a permanent Indian settlement at the base of the rocks as long as 7,000 years

GERALD S. RATLIFF

ago. Says archaeologist Ruth Brinker: "I imagine people came here then for many of the same reasons they come to this area now — for the fishing. the hunting and to be near the rocks."

Nature buries other wonders underground in Seneca Caverns and Smoke Hole Caverns. Indians used both as shelters from the weather and their enemies, as well as for important tribal events. The walls of the Ballroom chamber of Seneca Caverns are blackened with the soot of countless cooking fires. The Smoke Hole Caverns were used by the Indians to smoke their meat. During the Civil War. both

Dolly Sods is a naturalist's wonderland, offering scenes as diverse as swampy bogs and rocky barrens.

DAVID E. FATTALEH

A boardwalk threads its way through the forest at Cranberry Glades.

The view from Spruce Knob, the highest point in West Virginia.

GERALD S. RATLIFF ▶

The fishing doesn't stop when temperatures drop at Spruce Knob Lake.

Union and Confederate troops used the caves to store and hide ammunition. Legend has it that the soldiers also used the caves to hide treasure — gold bars, coins and other precious items — but none has ever been found. In later years, the caves were said to be home to more than one moonshine still.

The Monongahela National Forest is so vast that it virtually surrounds numerous state parks, state forests, public hunting areas and other attractions. These include Watoga State Park, Canaan Valley State Park, Blackwater Falls, the Cass Scenic Railroad and the National Radio Astronomy Observatory.

Watoga, in Pocahontas County, is the largest park in the extensive West Virginia state park system. Its 10,000 acres of woodland attract many return visitors each summer. Again, the hard-working members of the Depression-era CCC and WPA get the credit for building the park's sturdy log and stone cabins. In addition, Watoga offers more than 80 campsites. Riding fans can enjoy everything from 30-minute horseback jaunts to overnight trips into the park's remote areas.

The Canaan Valley is a 14-mile-long, five-mile-wide swath of rugged, mountainous terrain in Tucker County, the highest valley of its size east of the Rocky Mountains. In 1753, legend has

Tourists enjoy the view from Bald Knob, after riding Cass Scenic Railway to 4,300 feet elevation.

power in the strategic valley.

A small log museum at Droop Mountain State Park displays artifacts from the battle, which is re-enacted each October. But the best way to appreciate what happened there is to walk the park paths that lead to trenches and overlooks used by the Confederate troops and to the graves of those left behind by both sides.

Pocahontas County farm scene.

Sunrise over Mineral County highlights the mountainous terrain of West Virginia's eastern panhandle.

Opposite Page - The Potomac River, near Harpers Ferry.

Panhandle and Potomac Highlands

CHAPTER 10

Journalist John Gunther, writing in his 1940s classic, *Inside USA*, suggested that the geographic outline of West Virginia is rather like a squid. It is, as he observed, the only state with not one, but two panhandles. The heavily industrialized Northern Panhandle shoots up like an arrow between Ohio and Pennsylvania, coming to a point northwest of Pittsburgh. In contrast, the Eastern Panhandle is placid and rural — or, at least, that was the case until recently.

During the Civil War, the Eastern Panhandle included the tracks of the Baltimore and Ohio Railroad and thus controlled the all-important westerly approaches to Washington. Today,

those same railroad tracks have helped usher in a new chapter for the panhandle, one which sees it becoming a far-flung suburb of metropolitan Washington, D.C. In recent years, thousands of retirees, along with others who still hold 9-to-5 jobs but are willing to undertake a long daily commute, have flocked to Jefferson County in this easternmost tip of West Virginia. Many drive into the city each day — a 90-minute trip, not long by metropolitan Washington standards — but others take a daily commuter train.

The Eastern Panhandle's most famous town is legendary and picturesque Harpers Ferry, the scene of John Brown's famous 1859 raid and an appropriate

place to begin our look at the region.

In 1787, in his *Notes on the State of Virginia*, Thomas Jefferson described the view looking down from a high point behind Harpers Ferry. "On your right comes up the Shenandoah, having ranged along the foot of the mountain an hundred miles to seek a vent. On your left approaches the Potomac, in quest of a passage also. In the moment of their junction they rush together against the mountain, rend it asunder, and pass off to the sea."

It was, said Jefferson, a scene "worth a voyage across the Atlantic."

The Potomac River carves out the five counties of the

region. In Morgan County, the Cacapon River snakes northward to join it. Two branches of the Potomac meet above Paw Paw. The South Branch cuts through Hampshire County. The North Branch outlines Mineral County, where unusual rounded mountains, eroded by the long passage of time, stand like ceremonial mounds.

Harpers Ferry was first settled in 1732 by Peter Stephens. His rights were bought in 1747 by Robert Harper, for whom the town was named and who first operated ferries there across the Shenandoah and the Potomac. In 1794, President George Washington asked Congress to build an arsenal at Harpers Ferry, and construction

Railroading has been crucial to the Eastern Panhandle since before the Civil War. This is the old B&O bridge from Maryland to Harpers Ferry.

Thomas Jefferson said that the view down the Potomac River gap from above Harpers Ferry (right) was worth a trip across the ocean. His vantage point (below) is now known as Jefferson's Rock.

started two years later. This was the arsenal that would bring John Brown to Harpers Ferry.

A fiery abolitionist, Brown had played a major role in the bloody conflict between free-state and pro-slavery groups in Kansas. In the summer of 1859, with a small armed band of blacks and whites, he set up a military-like headquarters in a rented farmhouse near Harpers Ferry. There, he plotted a takeover of the town's arsenal, a step he was convinced would trigger a widespread slave revolt.

Launching his attack on the night of October 16, Brown quickly took the arsenal. Throughout the next day and night, he and his men held off the local militia. But the following morning he surrendered to a small force of U.S. Marines, ironically commanded by Colonel Robert E. Lee, the future Confederate general. Brown was jailed in nearby Charles Town and tried for murder, slave insurrection and treason. He was convicted and, on December 2, was hanged.

Brown failed in his attempt to incite a general slave uprising, but his raid had important consequences in greatly heightening the sectional animosities that soon would produce the Civil War. Northern intellectuals, including Ralph Waldo Emerson and Henry David Thoreau, looked upon Brown as a martyr.

John Brown's 1859 raid ended in the bloody siege of the tiny brick building known ever after as John Brown's Fort. Brown (below) was soon hanged at Charles Town, moving the nation toward civil war.

Harpers Ferry is a place of narrow streets and old brick and stone.

Some had bankrolled his ill-fated enterprise. When war came, Union soldiers took up the song "John Brown's Body," and his soul went "marching on."

Harpers Ferry became a National Historical Park in 1944, and each year the place attracts more than a half million visitors. In the John Brown Museum, visitors can see his Bible and sword, among other artifacts. The 19th Century Industries Museum includes gun-making machines of the type once used at the arsenal. In recent years, the National Park Service has restored a 19th Century clothing shop, rebuilt a jeweler's store, added black history displays and established nearby hiking trails.

The Appalachian Trail crosses the Potomac into West Virginia at Harpers Ferry on a new footbridge built across an old railroad bridge. Trail headquarters is at the corner of Washington and Jackson Streets, uphill from the park. The trail soon leaves West Virginia across the Shenandoah River opposite Harpers Ferry. It briefly touches the state again to the far south, in Monroe County.

Not far from Harpers Ferry is Shepherdstown, which claims to be both the oldest town in West Virginia and the birthplace of the steamboat. The town started out as Mecklenburg in 1762, was renamed Shepherd's Town in 1798 in honor of

Zion Episcopal Church and the Jefferson County Courthouse (above) are among Charles Town's historic landmarks.

The James Rumsey Memorial stands on the banks of the Potomac River at Shepherdstown.

founder Thomas Shepherd and became Shepherdstown in 1867, when it was granted a charter by the new state of West Virginia.

During the Revolutionary War, Shepherdstown was the jumping-off point for the legendary Bee Line March, in which the first large contingent of southern volunteers tramped overland to reinforce George Washington's fledgling Continental Army around Boston.

People elsewhere may think that Robert Fulton invented the steamboat. Not so, say folks in Shepherdstown. A monument there honors James Rumsey, who in 1787 — 20 years before Fulton's *Claremont* steamed up the Hudson River —

built and successfully demonstrated a working steamboat on the Potomac just below the cliff where the monument stands. But Rumsey died before he could raise the money needed to put his boat into commercial service, and so it was Fulton's name that went into the history books.

The Civil War never quite came to Shepherdstown, but the bloody Battle of Antietam was fought less than five miles away across the Potomac. After that battle, Shepherdstown became an impromptu hospital for the retreating Confederates.

When the county seat of Jefferson County was moved from Shepherdstown to Charles Town in 1871, the people in the area

Henry Louis Gates, Jr.

It's a long and challenging road from Mineral County to Harvard University, but that's the road Henry Louis Gates Jr. has traveled.

Gates, chairman of Afro-American Studies and the W.E.B. Du Bois Professor of Humanities at Harvard, was born in Keyser in 1950 and grew up in nearby Piedmont. In his intimate memoir, *Colored People*, he writes about what it was like to grow up black in the 1950s and '60s in the segregated Potomac Valley mill town.

Piedmont is a hard-working, blue-collar town, and Gates recalls his years there with wry affection. It was a "sepia time," he writes in *Colored People*, an era now irretrievably lost but well worth remembering. "Piedmont was prosperous and growing, a village of undoubted splendors," he says of his youth there. "People from Piedmont were always proud to be from Piedmont — nestled against a wall of mountains, smack-dab on the banks of the mighty Potomac. We knew God gave America no more beautiful location."

His father worked during the day as a paper-mill loader and at night moonlighted as a janitor. In 1957, when he was in elementary school, his mother became the first black secretary of the school's PTA.

In the late 1960s, young Gates mounted a campaign to close a local restaurant that held segregated dances on Saturday nights. His efforts made him less than popular, he recalls. "I was called `nigger' so often I thought I had a sign stenciled on my back."

In 1969, after spending a year at a local junior college, Gates entered Yale University. Moving from tiny Piedmont, with its population of 2,000, to the cosmopolitan environs of New Haven, Connecticut, was a dramatic change for him. "I encountered the most black people I had come across in one place in my life. It's ironic that one would go to Yale to learn about blackness."

Known to his friends as "Skip," Gates received a bachelor's degree in history from Yale University in 1973 and a doctorate in English from Cambridge University in 1979, becoming the first black American to receive a Ph.D. degree in that school's 800-year history. He worked for *Time* magazine in its London bureau and taught English and Afro-American Studies at Yale. Later he taught at Cornell University and still later at Duke University. He joined the Harvard faculty in 1991.

Through his years in academic life, Gates has argued that the American educational canon must be enlarged to include the study of the great works produced by non-Western cultures as well as those of Western Civilization. "What I advocate is a more truly diverse notion of excellence," he explains.

Gates received an honorary degree from West Virginia

"Skip" Gates is a distinguished son of Mineral County.

University in 1990, and was named West Virginian of the Year in 1994 by the *Charleston Sunday Gazette-Mail*. He attended Potomac State College for a brief period prior to attending Yale, and was honored with Potomac State's Distinguished Alumni Award in 1991.

His many other awards include the 1989 American Book Award for his *The Signifying Monkey: A Theory of African-American Literary Criticism* and the John D. and Catherine T. MacArthur Foundation's prestigious "genius award."

New Creek, near the town of New Creek, in Mineral County.

The Potomac Valley, as viewed from Prospect Peak in Morgan County.

decided to use the vacant courthouse for educational purposes. Incorporation papers for a school to be known as Shepherd College, designed to instruct students "in languages, arts and sciences," was drawn up by a board of trustees. Principal Joseph McMurran and two assistant professors were hired to teach the 41 students who began classes that September. The next year Shepherd became part of the state system.

Physical and academic growth have characterized Shepherd College's history since the mid-1960s. Twelve new buildings have been added to the campus, and the enrollment has grown from 1,100 students to 3,600. The college now offers academic programs in 70 different fields. In additon to its 323-acre campus in Shepherdstown, the school maintains a facility in Petersburg to serve the educational needs of the residents of the South Branch Valley.

A stroll through today's Shepherdstown (population 1,800) reveals several fine old homes, including some that predate the Revolution, and a number of historic 18th and 19th Century public buildings. The Old Market House, built in 1800, has served the community in various roles. Since 1922, it has been the town's library. The German Street Market has

The Bavarian Inn offers gracious hospitality reminiscent of past times in Jefferson County.

Apples are big business in West Virginia's Eastern Panhandle, filling orchard bins (bottom) and the weathered hands of harvest workers.

GERALD S. RATLIFF

provided Shepherdstown with groceries since 1791. The Opera House, built in 1909, is one of the oldest movie theaters in the nation and one of the first to make the transition from silent movies to "talkies." It closed in 1958 but, like much of Shepherdstown, has since been restored to its former grandeur. It now shows foreign and art films.

Today, the commercial and cultural hub of the Eastern Panhandle is Martinsburg. Laid out in 1773 by General Adam Stephen as a manufacturing center along Tuscarora Creek, it was incorporated in 1778. But it was the coming of the Baltimore & Ohio Railroad that put Martinsburg on the map.

Martinsburg's station, round-house, shops and other facilities were completed in 1849.

With the coming of the Civil War, the Union and the Confederacy struggled for control of the B&O. Raiding Confederate troops pried the rails loose and, heating them white hot, bent them around nearby trees. They burned the locomotives and rolling stock, and blasted bridges with dynamite. Then, Union troops would methodically rebuild the line — until the next Confederate raid.

All of the B&O buildings in Martinsburg were destroyed during the Civil War but were rebuilt in 1866. Today, the old B&O ticket station and the

Postcard view of historic Martinsburg, early 1900s.

Railroad Hotel are being renovated at a cost of nearly $1 million. In addition to preserving an important historic landmark, the project also will improve a vital part of the region's transportation system. Plans for the refurbished facility include ticketing services for commuters and other Amtrak passengers, an intermodal terminal for the interchange of bus and rail passengers, and plenty of parking.

Martinsburg has a wealth of historic and architecturally significant buildings, many built after 1890 when electricity arrived and sparked the town's development as a textile center.

The General Adam

Stephen House at 309 East John Street was built by the city's founder between 1774 and 1789. The two-story stone house was donated to the city in 1959, and a non-profit group organized to restore and furnish it. It is open to the public on weekends from May through October.

A handsome brick building at 208 South Queen Street is another of the oldest in the city. It was built sometime around 1802 by Philip Nadenbousch, who operated it as stagecoach stop. In 1832, it was sold to Charles Boarman, a commodore in the U.S. Navy. When he died in 1879, his distinguished naval career had spanned 68 years and three wars — the War of 1812,

the Mexican-American War and the Civil War. Today the building houses the Boarman Arts Center, which provides art exhibits and classes. On display at the center is the ship's log of the U.S. frigate *Brandywine*, one of several ships Boarman commanded during his long career. The log includes this entry from June 9, 1849 — "At sunset discovered Benj. Chambers (OS) dead on the birth [sic] deck, having died from a too free use of ardent spirits while on liberty."

At 126 East Race Street is the Belle Boyd House, home of the Confederacy's most famous spy, Isabella (Belle) Boyd. Born at Bunker Hill in Berkeley County, Belle Boyd spent most of her

childhood and adolescent years in Martinsburg. During this period she lived in several different houses. The house on Race Street is not the house where she shot and killed a Union soldier who was trying to take her mother's Confederate flag, but the one where Belle, a headstrong young girl, rode her pony through the front door after her father told her she was too young to attend a dinner party. In her autobiography, "In Camp and In Prison," Belle Boyd claimed to have passed Union military secrets to Stonewall Jackson a number of times during his 1862 Valley Campaign. Arrested as a spy, she was banished from the country. She returned to the United States in

The red brick buildings of Martinsburg's 19th century industrial era have been recycled as outlet stores.

The General Adam Stephen House, built in the 18th century, was the home of Martinsburg's founder.

The Belle Boyd house (right) recalls the exploits of the notorious Confederate spy.

1868, and spent the rest of her life as an actress in a traveling show. Today, her Race Street home is headquarters of the Berkeley County Historical Society.

Another Martinsburg point of interest is the Berkeley County Courthouse. Built 1855-56, it incorporates a smaller courthouse built on the same site in the 18th Century. Pressed tin ceilings, as well as original lighting fixtures, iron vaults and hardware still grace the interior. It was here that Belle Boyd was held after her arrest as a spy.

And then there's the Apollo Theater. Designed by Reginald Geare, architect for the famed Knickerbocker Theater in Washington, the Apollo first opened its doors in 1912. Over the years it has offered vaudeville performances, stage productions and movies. It now serves as a community theater.

But it's not just history that lures visitors to

Downtown Berkeley Springs exuded small town charm at the time this postcard view was made, and it still does today.

▲ STEPHEN J. SHALUTA, JR. ▼

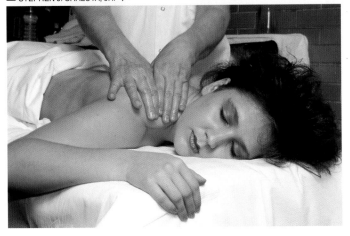

Historic Berkeley Springs (above) is one of West Virginia's oldest spas. Visitors still enjoy soaking in the mineral waters, followed by a soothing rubdown.

Martinsburg. The town is home to the Blue Ridge Outlet Center, a favorite destination for shoppers seeking brand-name and designer products at bargain prices. More than 50 shops with everything from apparel to housewares are housed in four refurbished buildings that once were textile factories.

Farther northwest along the Potomac lies Morgan County and Berkeley Springs. Berkeley Springs can not only boast that "Washington Slept Here," it can also claim that "Washington Bathed Here." Often. The nation's first president praised the therapeutic qualities of the water that bubbles to the surface at the springs. Now, at four and a

The South Fork of the South Branch is among the Potomac River's most remote tributaries.

Hardy Countians open their homes during the annual Heritage Weekend.

half acres, the site is the smallest state park in West Virginia.

Actually, long before the first Europeans discovered the waters of Berkeley Springs, the place attracted Indians from as far as the Great Lakes and the Carolinas. And it was the natives who introduced the first settlers to the springs. Washington was only 16 years old when he first visited the springs as part of a surveying party. The party camped at Berkeley Springs for the night, and young Washington wrote in his diary: "March 18th, 1748. We this day called to see Ye Fam'd Warm Springs." Washington's biographers report he visited the springs a total of eight times, twice as president,

Of Chickens and Eagles

A 52-mile stretch of railroad track runs through eastern West Virginia, from Green Spring to Petersburg. Officially, it is named the South Branch Valley Railroad. But virtually everybody calls it the "chicken railroad." The poultry industry fuels the local economy, and the trains of the South Branch mostly carry chicken feed.

In 1978, it looked like the end of the line for the South Branch. Its owner, the Chessie System's Baltimore & Ohio Railroad, insisted it no longer could ignore the short line's operating losses. The B&O proposed to shut it down. Poultry operators protested that an end to rail service would put them out of business, that they couldn't afford to pay the higher costs of having feed trucked in.

Worried about losing hundreds of jobs in Hardy, Hampshire and Grant counties, local government officials and business leaders took their case to Jay Rockefeller, then governor of West Virginia. Rockefeller in turn pleaded their cause to the Chessie System, which agreed to donate the line to the state.

Since then, state government has successfully operated the railroad, hauling tons of feed to millions of chickens every year. Not only was the region's poultry industry saved, it has expanded significantly in recent years.

The state-owned "chicken railroad" runs only Mondays through Fridays. On summer weekends since 1992, its tracks have been used by the *Potomac Eagle*, a sightseeing train operated by a private business, which pays the state a percentage of its revenues. The train is made up of restored railroad passenger cars from the 1920s.

A ride on the Potomac Eagle is a trip through some of the most beautiful scenery in the eastern United States. The train leaves a siding on the outskirts of Romney and passes through carefully tended farmland that has been tilled since before the Revolutionary War.

The highlight of the ride is a seven-mile stretch of track through The Trough, a canyon wide enough only for the river and the

The Potomac Eagle travels the South Branch.

railroad. Here, on most trips, the Potomac Eagle's passengers have a chance to see what the train is named for — bald eagles that nest in the canyon. The high valley walls and clear river water provide the seclusion and excellent fishing the eagles require.

STEPHEN J. SHALUTA, JR.

GERALD S. RATLIFF

Lyons Mill recalls a time of water power and simpler living in the Potomac Highlands.

Diners enjoy hearty country cooking (left) at Coolfont Resort in Berkeley County.

DAVID E. FATTALEH

The famous Berkeley Springs castle is an architectural curiosity, with a story to match.

and, like many prominent colonists, even bought a small home there. In future years, Presidents Madison, Polk, Filmore, Van Buren and Franklin Roosevelt also visited the springs.

Today, visitors continue to use and enjoy the springs, soaking their aches — and their troubles — away in spring waters swirling at a pain-soothing 102 degrees.

When not relaxing in the tub, visitors can find lots of other things to do in Berkeley Springs. There are several bed and breakfast establishments. The Country Inn, a sprawling historic lodging, adjoins the park. And there are antique shops, craft stores and restaurants.

Outside the town, there are other spas and resorts, including Coolfont Resort. A few miles south on U.S. 522 is Cacapon Resort State Park, which includes a huge lodge, an old inn (another legacy from the Civilian Conservation Corps) and an 18-hole championship golf course designed by Robert Trent Jones.

In its early days, Berkeley Springs enjoyed a reputation not only for its healthy waters but also as a place to have a good time. By the late 1800s, it boasted several gambling casinos, prompting a visiting Methodist minister to lament that the town "was good for the health, but most injurious to religion."

Parties were commonplace,

Hampshire County's Little Mountain is plenty big for a grand view of the surrounding countryside.

The old skills are still treasured in the panhandle. These quilters work in the community of Arkansas in Hardy County.

and none more lavish than those held at Berkeley Castle, a scaled-down replica of a Norman castle built on a hill above the town.

The castle was built by a wealthy Maryland businessmen in his 50s to persuade a debu-tante in her 20s to marry him. Constructing the castle, from huge blocks of hand-cut West Virginia sandstone, took three years and Colonel Samuel Taylor Suit died before it was com-pleted. In his will, he directed his young wife, Rosa, to finish the castle, which she did in 1885, using much of the $1 million in stocks and bonds he left her. The rest she spent on a series of opulent parties the likes of which Morgan County had

never seen. She rented private railroad cars to bring guests from Washington to the castle, where they danced the night away at parties that went on until dawn. Spending lavishly, Rosa ran through the colonel's money and, after selling off her fancy furniture piece by piece, lost the castle. She spent her last years on a small farm nearby, raising chickens.

Today, the partially restored castle — with its large stone-walled ballroom, wide carved staircase and tower room — is open daily for self-guided tours. The looming landmark is used for private parties, wedding receptions and an occasional murder-mystery weekend.

West Virginia: Mountains of Opportunity

GERALD S. RATLIFF

Continued growth.

That, the experts say, is the outlook for the West Virginia economy between now and 2005.

A report from the West Virginia University Center for Economic Research envisions that the state will continue adding jobs, population and real income in the decade ahead. Put another way, the center predicts that West Virginia in 2005 will have more jobs, more people and higher wages.

That's good news, and it comes as no surprise to those who have been following the many dramatic changes that have unfolded in the Mountain State in recent years.

West Virginia is experiencing impressive, measurable economic growth. In May, 1995, the PNC Banc Corporation cited West Virginia as being the fastest growing state in a nine-state region. Then, in June, *The Wall Street Journal* published a report quoting The Wefa Group index that found West Virginia to be second in the nation in economic growth. The state's unemployment rate for the first half of 1995 was the lowest since 1979. Real personal income in West Virginia over the past five years has consistently outpaced the national average.

The West Virginia Council for Community and Economic Development, created by the 1992 Legislature to provide oversight and direction to the state's economic development effort, reports that a record number of companies are expanding in West Virginia or moving to the state.

It's not hard to see why all these good things are happening.

Today's West Virginia boasts a competitive business climate, with an attractive package of job-luring tax credits. We're a national leader in education and rural health, and we're home to the nation's premier telecommunications network. Proud, dedicated West Virginia workers — the best to be found anywhere — live and work surrounded by natural beauty and unmatched recreational opportunities. Combine these qualities with the lowest crime rate in the nation, and West Virginia truly is "Almost Heaven."

Little wonder that West Virginia is on the move.

WVU's Center for Economic Research forecasts that jobs in West Virginia will increase at a rate of 10,300 a year through 2005. This growth will be concentrated in the service-producing sector of the economy. Continued gains in population and jobs will bring steady job growth to the construction industry.

On the whole, the growth rate of employment in West Virginia is forecast to equal, or exceed, the national employment growth rate. This shows that West Virginia has mostly adjusted to the structural shifts which hit the state during the years 1979-1983, when dramatic productivity gains resulted in employment declines in mining and manufacturing.

The WVU Center envisions continued output growth in all sectors of the state economy, including mining and manufacturing. Real gross state product is seen increasing an average of 2.1 percent a year in the economy's service-producing sector and an average of 1.6 percent a year in the goods-producing sector.

Output growth will be vigorous in such key industries as chemicals, machinery and wood products. Mining, manufacturing and construction will continue to be important to the West Virginia economy in the decade now unfolding.

Population in West Virginia is forecast to increase by 6,000 people a year. The 45-and-older age group will gain the most and will make up 41 percent of the state's population by 2005.

And most types of per capita income are expected to continue growing as quickly, or more quickly, in West Virginia than nationally.

A number of factors, when added up, combine to make West Virginia a state with Mountains of Opportunity. Let's take a closer look at some of them.

Location! Location! Location!

West Virginia is located within 500

WV COUNCIL FOR COMMUNITY AND ECONOMIC DEVELOPMENT

Ohio River waterfront improvements.

GERALD S. RATLIFF

Interstate 79, Mercer County.

miles — roughly a day's drive — of two-thirds of the U.S. population and one-third of Canada's population. The 22 states within a 500-mile radius of West Virginia are the scene of more than half the manufacturing activity in the United States.

An efficient transportation network, including one of the nation's newest interstate systems, enables West Virginia to take full advantage of that strategic location.

Cincinnati, Columbus, Pittsburgh, Washington, D.C., and many other major cities are only a few hours away by one of the half-dozen interstate highways that crisscross West Virginia. Interstates 70, 68 and 64 link east and west, while Interstates 77, 79 and 81 carry north-south traffic. In addition, the Appalachian corridor system, when complete, will bring modern, divided, four-lane expressways to much more of West Virginia.

With two major airports — Yeager Airport in Charleston and Tri-State Airport in Huntington — and other smaller airports around the state, West Virginia is no more than one stop away from every major city in the world. It's also worth noting that in most cases a short commuter flight from any city in West Virginia takes less time than a drive across town to the airport in many of the nation's big cities.

Rivers and railroads played tremendously important roles in the history of West Virginia and today they make cargo delivery to and from West Virginia an easy, inexpensive proposition.

West Virginia has more than 400 miles of navigable rivers — the Ohio, the Kanawha, the Monongahela and the Big Sandy. Eighteen of West Virginia's 55 counties, representing 53 percent of the state population, have direct access to waterways. The Port of Huntington, with its many facilities for loading West Virginia coal onto Ohio River barges, is one of the nation's busiest inland ports.

West Virginia's 2,600 miles of railway are served by three railroads — CSX Transportation, Conrail and Norfolk Southern. In addition, passenger rail service is offered by Amtrak and Maryland Rail Commuter Service.

A nighttime view of Union Carbide, ARCO Chemical and Rhone-Poulenc at Institute.

West Virginia's unsurpassed access to North American markets has played a key role in the state's continued growth as an exporter. Among the 50 states, West Virginia is the sixth largest exporter of goods and services, with gross annual export sales of more than $4 billion a year.

These advantages of location played an important role in convincing NGK Spark Plug Manufacturing (USA) Inc. to construct a new oxygen sensor plant near Charleston. Japan-based NGK is an example of the companies the state's trade office in Nagoya, Japan, works to bring to West Virginia.

The state's Warehouse Freeport Tax Exemption Amendment provides attractive incentives for business to locate in West Virginia. Goods in transit to an out-of-state destination are exempt from ad valorem property taxes when warehoused in West Virginia. Many leading companies, including AT&T, General Motors, Norm Thompson and Rite Aid, have recognized the state's strategic location and have situated major warehousing complexes to serve multi-state areas from West Virginia.

Business Climate

West Virginia is a state with an understanding of business and a vision for the future, a state ready to provide companies with a wide range of meaningful assistance for growth and economic development.

The Business Investment and Jobs Expansion Tax Credit — often referred to as the "Super Tax Credit" — is one reason so many companies have chosen West Virginia. A business that creates 50 or more jobs can offset up to 80 percent of its basic state business tax liability for over 10 years through the Super Tax Credit. This innovative program is based on a formula calculated by using a job creation and qualified investment factor. The Super Tax Credit is available to all businesses, large and small, new or existing, that meet the basic criteria, keyed to payroll and gross sales.

The Corporate Relocation Credit is available to companies that relocate their corporate headquarters to West Virginia and create at least 15 new jobs. For example, if the relocation of a corporate headquarters results in 50 or more new jobs, the allowable credit is 50 percent of the adjusted qualified investment.

Adding to its positive business environment, West Virginia extends its incentive package to include:

— Below prime-rate financing participation for capital improvements to qualified companies. The West Virginia Economic Development Authority promotes job creation and economic development through a variety of financing programs.

Sparks fly at Steel of West Virginia.

— Infrastructure improvements consistently funded through an annual statutory dedication.

— A tax-exempt industrial revenue bond set-aside for eligible manufacturing facilities also makes provisions for smaller projects.

— A venture capital company tax credit that has established dozens of venture capital companies with a total investment pool of more than $100 million.

— The award-winning Governor's Guaranteed Work Force Program assists in an employer's needs with the best possible training solution and provides a fully trained work force.

— One-stop shopping for licensing makes going into business in West Virginia efficient and easy. Through one-stop registration, all appropriate agencies are notified of a new business, thereby becoming facilitators.

West Virginia is rich in natural resources. Because West Virginia is the second largest producer of coal in the United States, power companies are able to offer low rates. The state's industrial electrical rates are 25 percent below the national average. A wealth of natural gas also provides rates below the national average and enables West Virginia to be the largest natural gas producer east of the Mississippi.

With more than 12 million acres of timberland, a

©RICK LEE

three-to-one natural growth rate and 60 million board feet of inventory, West Virginia has attracted many of the biggest and best-known names in the wood industry. Companies such as Trus Joist MacMillan, Columbia Forest Products, Bruce Hardwood Floors, Georgia-Pacific Corporation, Pacific Encore East, Weyerhaeuser and Westvaco are investing, maintaining or constructing substantial production facilities within the state.

West Virginia's positive business environment has been praised by national financial publications, including *Business Week*, *Financial World* and *The Bond Buyer*. But perhaps Ray Smith, chairman and chief executive officer of Bell Atlantic Corporation, has said it best: "Aside from being a state with majestic scenery and honest, friendly people, West Virginia has one of the best business climates anywhere ... the list of economic advantages is pretty compelling."

Going High-Tech

West Virginia, looking to the future, offers a wide range of technological expertise and capabilities.

The state's extensive telecommunications infrastructure is among the most advanced in the nation. As one of only two states with 100 percent digital switching, West Virginia provides faster, clearer telephone transmission to its entire population. The availability of an integrated systems digital network enables businesses to transmit or receive voice, data and video simultaneously. And with more than 100,000 miles of fiber optic cable in place, West Virginia can ensure uninterrupted state-of-the-art telecommunication service to businesses throughout the state.

West Virginia has a growing capability to provide advanced techno-

©STEVE PAYNE

Profiles in Corporate Excellence

Petroleum Products

West Virginia-American Water Company

Jackson & Kelly, Attorneys at Law

Monongahela Power

Shawnee Hills, Inc.

Mountain State Blue Cross & Blue Shield

PETROLEUM PRODUCTS

I n the field, on the job, in the plant or on the road, West Virginia works with Petroleum Products! Since 1938, Petroleum Products, Inc. has brought quality fuels, lubricants, and service to the heart of West Virginia.

From service stations, to industrial sites, Petroleum Products' commitment to

service and product quality is unparalleled. PPI is a major distributor of Chevron, Ashland, Shell, Mobil, and Valvoline products. Our multiple lines and multimillion-dollar inventory guarantee PPI customers maximum choice, economy, and product availability. But it's service that adds true value to all our products.

At Petroleum Products, service is a promise - a tradition of concern for our customers that everyone in our organization understands. With PPI on your team, you've got a lot more than just product on your site. You've got service on your side. Service that includes oil analysis, lubricant surveys, tanks and pumps, training seminars for your personnel, 24-hour technical assistance, and on-site troubleshooting.

And Petroleum Products delivers, with the largest in-house petroleum fleet in Southern West Virginia and multiple warehouses throughout the region. With PPI,

you'll always get the product you need, when you need it, and service you can count on. Our commitment to service extends beyond the marketplace and into the community. We've made a home in West Virginia, and we're here to stay. That's why every PPI storage facility and on-site installation is designed with safety and the environment in mind. Regular safety-training seminars,

on-site spill response kits, DOT and MSHA driver certification, and in-house emergency response teams highlight PPI's environmental/safety program.

Over the last decade, Petroleum Products, Inc. has experienced substantial growth under the leadership of Pat Graney. Through careful acquisition and well-planned expansion, PPI managers built upon the company's historic

stability and existing resources. Despite an unwieldy economy and intense competition, Petroleum Products has enjoyed robust growth in sales each year since 1988. Today, PPI's capacity to meet new challenges and aggressively respond to change is reflected in its sustained growth and continued stability.

Professional management, dedication to service, quality products, and over fifty-five years of experience - that's Petroleum Products. At PPI our vision for the future is focused squarely on West Virginia. We intend to operate the best diversified petroleum distributorship in the region and are pledged to add value to every product we sell. With Petroleum Products, you'll get what you pay for and you'll receive service you can't put a price on. Take a close look at PPI...we're a better deal!

"When I bought into Petroleum Products in the early seventies, the oil business was in the midst of massive change. Throughout the decade and into the '80s we adapted our methods and our products to this roller coaster marketplace and managed to prosper. Sure it was tough, but through it all I never questioned our ability to succeed.

"Perhaps what inspired my confidence was a basic belief in our company, the capabilities of our employees, and the strength of our customer relationships. Strong relationships are built upon promises kept. And PPI has kept its promises with exceptional customer service.

"Into the '90s and beyond, PPI's shining star will continue to be service. We are determined to remain on the technological edge of the distribution business through better organization, more efficient operations, and new expertise. And although we will add new products and extend our current lines, our tradition of adding value to every product will remain unchanged. You can count on it!"
Patrick C. Graney, III
President

West Virginia-American Water Company

The beauty of water has mesmerized man for thousands of years. It is a natural wonder that cannot be manufactured. In the United States, a person can turn on the tap any time of the day or night, and it will appear . . . fresh . . . clean . . . reliable. Water is a precious gift and must be protected.

A community cannot exist, or enjoy economic growth without a safe, dependable source of supply for drinking water. The State of West Virginia is extremely fortunate to have a bountiful supply of clean water.

One business grateful for this natural blessing is West Virginia-American Water Company, an investor-owned subsidiary of the American Water Works Company,

strongly believes in community citizenship, company and personnel involvement, and a commitment to quality life. When WVAWC serves a community, it becomes a part of that community: Service doesn't stop with the delivery of water to the customer.

The Company has faithfully served potable water to West Virginians for over one hundred years. The three oldest systems

The Charleston Operations Center, which houses distribution, outside commercial, and leak detection.

Inc. WVAWC is the largest drinking water supplier in the state, deliver-ing over 17 billion gallons of water each year to approximately 25 percent of the population.

Drinking water at its best

WV-American provides water service to over 130 communities located in 12 counties. The Company's employees live and work in these towns and cities, serving as leaders, volunteers, coaches, church workers, and much more. WV-American

started water service in the late 1800s: Charleston in 1886; Huntington in 1887; and Bluefield in 1888. Two WV-American facilities are National Historic Water Landmarks — The Ada water treatment plant in Bluefield (Mercer County) and the 24th Street water treatment plant in Huntington (Cabell County). Maintenance is a keystone in the longevity and operation of treatment plants, booster stations, water storage tanks, etc. When water facilities are operated and maintained by WV-American, they last.

Pure West Virginia-American know how

WV-American is an industry leader in water quality and research. Professional chemists and microbiologists staff the water quality team and ensure all state and federal requirements are met; and, they look into the future to anticipate and prepare for new regulations. Members of the water quality staff are experts in their professions, fully aware of advanced technology and how to best serve the customer.

To augment what happens on the local scene, the American Water System staffs and maintains a water quality laboratory in Belleville, Ill. where drinking water specialists perform cutting-edge research and exotic tests. This lab enhances testing capability and is economical.

Private ownership is an advantage in many ways. Privatization helps the local economy by paying state gross receipts, property and other business taxes - taxes that assist in the support of community services and facilities. The need for public capital constantly exceeds the supply of money. An investor-owned water utility uses private capital to build and expand its system. Access to private capital eliminates the need to issue municipal bonds, and the need to rely on limited public capital to maintain a reliable and safe water supply.

The consumer benefits by drinking safe, high quality water, enjoying consistent water service, and paying lower insurance rates because they now have dependable fire protection. They have toll-free telephone access to a centralized

customer service department that is tops in performance, and a 24-hour emergency line that with one call will dispatch a distribution crew on an "as-needed" basis. Furthermore, when WV-American begins service to a new area, the price of water is reduced.

Single Tariff Pricing (STP), one rate for all customers, allows an affordability for quality water service that might otherwise be restricted due to the small number of customers on a system. STP permits WV-American the opportunity to provide smaller communities/systems with equal services and a high quality of water for the same or lesser price than their larger neighbors. STP is a major advantage for WVAWC customers.

The Kanawha Valley Water Treatment Plant in Charleston. It is home to production and water quality.

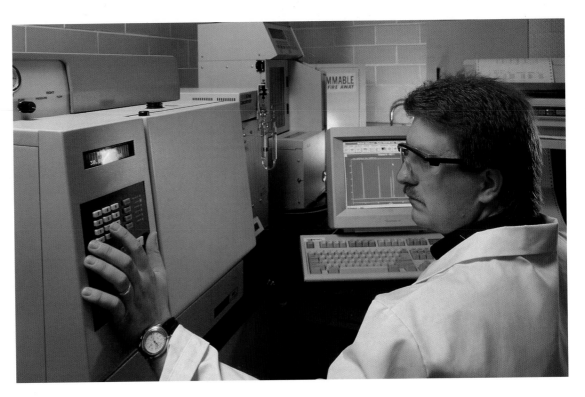

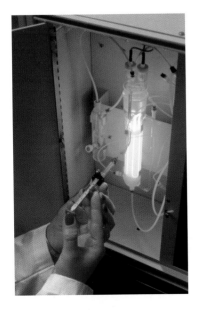

WV-American is a leader in providing water on a regional scale; and the Company actively encourages regionalization as the answer to developing water systems in the Mountain State. The focus must be on what is best for all concerned in the long-term and avoid the creation and continuation of small systems that simply cannot continue to function efficiently and at a cost that will no doubt become prohibitive in the absence of grants or "free" money.

The regionalization concept is to build one treatment plant that pumps water into a regional distribution system that can consist of hundreds of miles of mains. One advantage is economies-of-scale — lower chemical usage, reduced debt, less maintenance, and a high level of efficiency. Another advantage is building for the future and creating the opportunity for economic growth and area development. Since treatment plants and raw water intake structures are the most expensive part of a water system, regionalization just makes sense.

Another concept which works well for small projects and larger regionalization projects is the Public/Private Partnership. WV-American and various government agencies throughout the state have participated in public/private joint ventures since the late 1970s. Many of these projects affected thousands of people who did not have any type of water service, or those who were receiving poor quality water or water that violated standards; WVAWC is an advocate of the consumer's right for clean drinking water and reliable water service.

The objective in a public/ private venture is to bring water to all citizens while providing a basic infrastructure for economic development. Neither the public sector nor the private sector can accomplish all that needs to be done alone. Working together for the common good is the answer.

The largest Public/Private Partnership generated in the state is the Mercer/Summers Regional Water Project that is truly the best of both worlds. It is the second largest water project in the history of West Virginia. The largest was the construction of the 40 million gallons per day Charleston treatment plant, transmission lines, and relay stations in the early 1970s.

Enthusiasm, dedication, and selflessness have driven this classic endeavor from day one. There exists an unprecedented air of achievement . . . of what can be accomplished when everyone works together toward a shared goal . . . of how dreams can become realities.

The American Water System has the resources and abilities to invest additional equity in water and wastewater infrastructure. It is American's corporate policy to reinvest 25 percent of its earnings each year back into the state in which it operates. This policy is much better than most private water companies and affords WV-American the opportunity to have a very large part in helping solve water and wastewater needs in the Mountain State.

West Virginia-American Water Company knows the future is too important to leave to chance and that West Virginians need to plan and control their own destinies. Elements critical to success are progressive legislation, innovative thinking, cooperation, and the desire to develop West Virginia into a crown jewel of the South-East. West Virginia has all these elements and together we can make it work.

Kanawha Valley water treatment plant.

Jackson & Kelly, Attorneys at Law

It is not often that a major law firm is as well known and respected for its individual members' community involvement as for its members' professional excellence. Yet, that is a large part of the reputation Jackson & Kelly has developed over the years. As the largest law firm in West Virginia and one of the 250 largest firms in the

Senior partner Thomas E. Potter (center) celebrates the dedication of the Robert C. Byrd Cancer Research Laboratories at the Mary Babb Randolph Cancer Center in Morgantown with Senator Byrd and Mike Perry.

Serving as Chairman of the Board of Trustees at Thomas Memorial Hospital allows partner John R. Lukens (left) the opportunity to observe the latest technological acquisition with Hospital President Steve Dexter.

country, Jackson & Kelly has earned preeminent status through vigorous legal representation and an absolute commitment to the betterment of West Virginia, its home state.

Jackson & Kelly, West Virginia's oldest law firm, is a name historically synonymous with the practice of law. What started in 1822 as a firm involved in the affairs of the Commonwealth of Virginia and the events leading to the formation of West Virginia, including the First Constitutional Convention and early sessions of the Legislature, has since grown to a full-service law firm with some 140 attorneys practicing in several office locations. Throughout its history, Jackson & Kelly lawyers have been steadfast in their efforts to meet the needs of the various communities in which the lawyers practice.

Jackson & Kelly's practice includes virtually all areas of the law (refer to listing on the next page), and its lawyers have developed specialties in these areas. When a significant project

or challenge at any Jackson & Kelly office calls for diverse expertise, a team of appropriate specialists can be formed immediately from throughout the firm, thus bringing together the talent, knowledge and experience necessary to best serve each client. Much of the firm's strength lies in the breadth of its practice and knowledge base.

Although meeting the legal needs of myriad corporate and individual clients effectively and efficiently is of paramount concern, the firm maintains a strong tradition of public involvement through charitable generosity and participation in the arts and education. Several firm members have had a key role in the drafting of major legislation that has shaped and continues to shape the future of West Virginia. Individual lawyers donate substantial time and expertise to pro bono work, while others proudly advise and volunteer their services and support to many charitable, cultural, social, service, and civic organizations, and educational institutions. The tradition of excellence that has become the trademark of West Virginia's oldest and largest law firm is perhaps best exemplified in these areas of community and charitable service.

An emphasis on things that matter

Jackson & Kelly's reputation is based on much more than historical milestones and legal victories. Through its many lawyers and staff members, the spirit of community involvement is active and widespread, and volunteers by the dozens support a

variety of educational programs throughout the State. At every level of education - from early childhood to college - Jackson & Kelly personnel are ever present in supporting the various needs of West Virginia's schools. While much of this support is realized in terms of financial underpinnings for special programs, the level of personal involvement and commitment is by far the greatest resource provided.

Numerous individuals serve as tutors, judges for social studies and science fairs, and weekly readers with the Read Aloud West Virginia program. The firm regularly hosts student field trips in support of career education programs, offers internships in conjunction with nearby colleges and universities, and has provided resources to fund scholarships. Lawyers serve as adjunct faculty at both public and private colleges and universities, not only in West Virginia but in other geographic areas in which the firm is located. Several partners serve in leadership posts on the boards of trustees, advisory boards, visiting committees and foundation boards of many of these well-respected institutions, with particular emphasis at West Virginia University.

Of course, education cannot be confined to the boundaries of a school yard or campus. That is why the firm generously supported the creation of the Sunrise Museum Science Hall in Charleston. In its first year, this hands-on, children-oriented, interactive experience in the physical and health sciences exposed some 48,000 visitors and 12,000 school children to more than 30 exhibits

Jackson & Kelly's Managing Partner John L. McClaugherty regularly reads aloud to the second grade class at Piedmont Elementary School.

that demonstrate basic principles of light and color, energy and magnetism, illusion and perception, and art and architecture.

Along with a solid commitment to education, Jackson & Kelly's lawyers maintain a strong presence in areas of political, cultural, and industrial significance. The strength of the firm's support of these various organizations is again seen in the voluntary leadership roles assumed by individual firm members with groups and associations such as the YWCA and YMCA, the West Virginia Symphony, the National Institute for Chemical Studies, Sunrise Museum, and shelters for the homeless and abused women and children, to name a few. Many lawyers invest significant amounts of time volunteering for political efforts at the local, state and national levels, while others hold elected offices. Similarly, community development and improvement committees, churches, and youth athletic programs benefit greatly from Jackson & Kelly's numerous volunteers and leaders.

Jackson & Kelly is a committed community member in each and every city where it has an office, providing human and financial resources in support of the United Way and its many agencies, as well as numerous other community endeavors. The firm's lawyers are involved with more than 200 charitable organizations and business, cultural and civic associations in West Virginia alone. Combined with the community activities in the other cities in which firm offices are located, the depth of Jackson & Kelly's involvement is considerable.

A steady hand toward the future

With a strong desire to better serve its client base, Jackson & Kelly has carefully expanded by opening several regional offices beyond Charleston. While many of these offices are located throughout West Virginia, Jackson & Kelly has successfully expanded into Kentucky and Washington, DC, and most recently into Denver, Colorado. These communities have quickly learned what Jackson & Kelly's clients and West Virginians have known for some 175 years...Jackson & Kelly is deeply committed to the practice of law of the highest quality and totally involved with the communities its lawyers serve. To both of these commitments the firm brings innovation and productive change, backed by nothing less than the highest degree of personal integrity and professional excellence.

Areas of Practice

banking
bankruptcy
business & commercial
domestic relations
employee benefits
energy & natural resources
environmental
federal black lung
government contracts
health care
health & safety
insurance regulation
intellectual property
international trade
labor & employment
legislative services
litigation
mergers, acquisitions & transactions
offshore
public finance
public utilities
small business development
real estate
taxes, estates & trusts
white collar crime
workers' compensation

Monongahela Power

Monongahela Power began serving customers in north central West Virginia and southeastern Ohio more than 100 years ago, but the electric utility is by no means an ancient relic.

Rather, Monongahela is building on its time-honored reputation as a reliable provider of low-cost electric service to meet the growing demands of a newly competitive era in the electric utility industry. As government officials prepare to deregulate the once-monopolistic business, Monongahela is modifying its operations and strengthening its market position to more carefully focus on its customers and their needs.

Rooted In the region

The company has its roots in the mid-Ohio Valley at Parkersburg, where the first electric company that was to become Monongahela was founded in 1886. That company, which provided streetlighting and, eventually, streetcar service, later became the Kanawha Valley Traction Company.

Today, Monongahela, headquartered in Fairmont, is part of Allegheny Power along with Potomac Edison, located in Hagerstown, Md., and West Penn Power in Greensburg, Pa.

Allegheny Power also owns the Allegheny Power Service Corporation, which provides staff services to the three operating units, and the Allegheny Generating Company, which holds the system's share of the Bath County hydroelectric plant in Bath County, Va. A new subsidiary, AYP Capital, is exploring growth areas in the electric utility industry.

Located in the heart of the coal fields

Monongahela has been able to maintain its low cost of service throughout the years mostly because its generating facilities are located in the rich coal fields of the region. With six power plants in Harrison, Marion, Monongalia, Pleasants and Preston counties, Monongahela has abundant generation to meet the growing needs of its service territory through the year 2010 and beyond.

The company's service centers are strategically located in Clarksburg, Elkins, Fairmont, Gassaway, Morgantown, Parkersburg, Weirton and Marietta, Ohio, to provide quick, quality service to its more than 343,000 residential, commercial and industrial customers. A convenient customer service center is also accessible by telephone.

Committed to the environment

Dedicated to good environmental stewardship, Monongahela and its sister organizations recently installed a flue gas desulfurization system, or scrubbers, on their largest generating plant, Harrison Power Station, located near Shinnston. One of the largest projects of its kind in North America during construction, the scrubbers take enough sulfur dioxide out of the plant's emissions to keep all of Allegheny Power in compliance with the Clean Air Act Amendments of 1990.

Dedicated To Safety

One area that will not change for Monongahela in the new competitive arena is its dedication to safety. Monongahela's nearly 2,000 employees have one of the most exemplary work records in the industry and will continue to make safe work practices their leading goal. As testimony to this safety record, Allegheny Power's coveted Presidental Safety Award, given for five years or 1 million hours without a lost workday accident, has been won by Monongahela employees 20 times since the award's inception in 1990.

Company officials are constantly striving to find ways to provide better quality and reliable service to Monongahela customers, who, in turn, enjoy some of the lowest electric rates in the country. As talk of deregulation and competition continues to

Monongahela Power Co. linemen at work.

escalate, Monongahela will continue to shape and condition its business to meet the challenges of the new environment.

By combining more than 100 years' experience in the electric utility business with a new competitive attitude, Monongahela's entry into the 21st Century should be a smooth transition.

Harrison Power Station, Haywood, W.Va., is APS's largest generating station.

Shawnee Hills, Inc.

Founded more than 20 years ago to serve the needs of the mentally disabled, Shawnee Hills, Inc. has established itself as a leader in behavioral health-care services and is the area's premier service provider for children and families, individuals, and the business community.

Decades of growth

Since it began in 1973, Shawnee Hills has experienced both programmatic and financial growth. From a small center serving 75 mentally retarded individuals, Shawnee Hills has expanded to a multi-facility operation serving over 14,000 individuals and families in 1995. Those served also includes individuals with mental health or substance abuse problems.

Group, a related business which employees handicapped individuals in competitive community jobs.

Changed funding streams

The overall operating budget has grown from $240,000 in 1973 to over $45 million in 1995. As have other service agencies, Shawnee Hills has moved from charities and grant writing through contracting with the state and other fee-for-service reimbursement

as Total Quality Management, leadership development, and strategic planning.

Such diversification has helped to support the direct service components of Shawnee Hills and allowed the social purpose to remain a central focus when planning business operations.

Awards & recognition

Shawnee Hills is accredited by the Joint Commission and has received numerous local, state and national awards for excellence and social contribution.

In 1995, Shawnee Hills received the Award of Excellence, National Council of Community MH Centers; "Expect the Best Award;" WV Chamber of Commerce; "Innovative Funding for Social Mission" Award (Business Development), National Community Mental Healthcare Council, and President's Award for Excellence in Risk Management, J.J. Negley.

Although the main office is in downtown Charleston, Shawnee Hills provides services statewide. In addition to operating programs in six counties, the organization has formed working partnerships with other related community agencies throughout West Virginia and in serveral other states. Shawnee Hills is nationally recognized as a leader in service excellence, total quality management, and leadership development.

Contribution to the community

In addition to providing much needed services, the growth of Shawnee Hills has contributed to the economic well-being of the state as a whole and to numerous local communities. In the past two decades, the organization has grown from 22 employees to over 1,100 full-time and 250 part-time staff within the organization proper. An additional 750 are employed through corporations managed by Shawnee Hills and/or through the Diversified Business

systems into funding through managed care competition.

Mission and values

Although the original mission to serve the disabled has not changed, it has expanded beyond the role of direct care provider. Shawnee Hills has entered into business ventures ranging from contracting to provide management services to offering a training and consulting business, S.H. Visions Unlimited, Inc. Since 1992, Visions has become recognized nationally as a leader in areas such

Looking to the future

As a part of today's national health-care reform, Shawnee Hills is quickly moving into the managed care arena. Through partnerships with other providers locally, statewide, and nationally the organization will remain an integral player.

Shawnee Hills was built on the belief that obstacles and difficulties are merely challenges to be overcome. With this attitude and recognition of the need to prepare for, rather than react to, change and to embrace the opportunities it presents, the organization looks forward to the future.

Mountain State Blue Cross & Blue Shield

As the outgrowth of the second-oldest Blue Cross plan in the nation, Mountain State Blue Cross & Blue Shield has a long legacy of providing quality health care coverage for a reasonable cost. It began on December 20, 1932, when John Hart made history by forming Hospital

Gregory K. Smith, company president since May 1995, oversees the operation of Mountain State Blue Cross & Blue Shield from its Parkersburg headquarters.

Customer Service Team Member Lois Rice answers member questions from Mountain State's customer service center in Wheeling.

Service Inc. to provide hospitalization coverage to Charleston area residents — the second such plan in the country. Also in the 1930s, Parkersburg Hospital Service Inc. was created to provide hospitalization, and Medical Surgical Care was founded to provide medical and surgical coverage. The Charleston and Parkersburg plans eventually became the only two Blue Cross and Blue Shield plans in the state.

Hart started the Charleston company on a shoestring budget with a $120 cash advance and a line of credit of $150 with each local hospital. The plan grew as the concept of health insurance caught on and in 1994 Mountain State reported total revenues of more than $318 million.

Mountain State is the successor to a heritage of West Virginia Blue Cross and Blue Shield organizations located in Huntington, Fairmont, Bluefield, Clarksburg, Wheeling, Parkersburg, Charleston and Morgantown. The companies began a series of mergers and consolidations that continued until 1984, leaving two Blue Cross and Blue Shield plans in the state — one in Charleston and one in Parkersburg.

In late 1990, Parkersburg's Blue Cross & Blue Shield of West Central West Virginia Inc. and Blue Cross & Blue Shield of Ohio, based in Cleveland, affiliated, moving Charleston's Blue Cross & Blue Shield of West Virginia Inc. book of business to the Parkersburg plan, creating Mountain State Blue Cross & Blue Shield.

Despite its growth, the headquarters remain in tranquil Parkersburg. A part of West Virginia's rich history, the company and its predecessor corporations have played a vital role in health care in West Virginia.

The early prepaid hospitalization and medical programs of the 1930s were the forerunners of health insurance, based on the concept of paying small monthly fees that would be used to pay for care in the event of illness or injury.

In those early days, Blue Cross and Blue Shield plans were the only options for those seeking shelter from the financial burdens of medical bills. Blue Cross plans covered hospitalization, while Blue Shield plans paid doctors. Eventually, Blue Cross and Blue Shield joined forces to provide total health coverage.

Today, Mountain State is the only health insurance company operating under the famous Blue Cross and Blue Shield logos in West Virginia. And, it is the only major health insurance company headquartered here.

From its humble beginnings to its current stature as West Virginia's largest health insurance carrier, Mountain State has continually evolved since 1932. Its current business philosophy mirrors its

founder's — to provide solid coverage as inexpensively as possible. In the 1940s, some of the company's first advertisements touted its low administrative costs — less than 10 cents of every revenue dollar. That fact has not changed. Mountain State continues its commitment to West Virginians to have the lowest cost of doing business of any major health insurance carrier in the state.

Covering West Virginia

Mountain State serves all of West Virginia's 55 counties plus border counties in Ohio, Pennsylvania, Kentucky, Virginia and Maryland. The company provides or administers health coverage for nearly 300,000 people.

The company serves a myriad of commercial and governmental customers through its diverse products. Its success has been built upon Mountain State's positive relationship with health care providers. The company maintains a comprehensive network of providers and offers a choice of many hospitals, physicians and medical professionals to both its traditional and managed care customers.

This philosophy of basing coverage on a provider network dates back to early Blue Cross founder John Hart's strategy in 1932: he persuaded Charleston's six hospitals to accept Blue Cross payment for services.

Customer service

Mountain State has always based its corporate identity on excellent customer service.

From its dedicated customer service team to an efficient claims processing unit, the company's strength is its more than 485

employees with a commitment to its members. Mountain State processes more than 2.4 million claims each year, 230,000 of them for federal employees' Blue Cross and Blue Shield coverage and another 18,000 for Mountain State's Public Employees Insurance Agency managed care program. Mountain State also processes hundreds of thousands of claims for West Virginia's top industries, including steel corporations, natural gas companies and coal organizations.

Lori Binkiewicz and her co-workers in Mountain State's Wheeling office process 2.4 million claims each year.

A winning team

In addition to a group of committed employees, Mountain State's team includes physicians in more than 7,300 locations. This network features 300 primary care physicians who direct the health care of customers covered by Mountain State's Super Blue® Select Point-of-Service product. Physicians in 3,800 locations serve the company's Super Blue® Plus Preferred Provider Organization.

Mountain State's team also includes 72 hospitals, 61 of which are available for managed care customers.

Products with a rich history

Mountain State strives to be a managed care leader, creating products to fulfill customer needs. The company develops its products to attain a delicate balance between individual choice and true cost savings.

With both choice and savings

in mind, Super Blue Plus came on line in 1994. A participating provider organization, Plus relies upon Mountain State's diverse provider network.

In 1993, Mountain State developed Super Blue Select for Weirton Steel Corporation. Select is a Point of Service product, which is similar to an HMO, but provides benefits even to customers who seek care outside the network.

In 1995, Mountain State began offering Super Blue Select to state employees covered by the Public Employees Insurance Agency. During 1994 and 1995, Select was developed and marketed for private sector groups.

While forging ahead to meet West Virginia's shifting health care requirements, Mountain State continues to acknowledge that some customers prefer traditional insurance programs. To serve these customers, Mountain State offers New Blue℠, a traditional indemnity health insurance plan, and continues to refine it to mesh with evolving needs.

Mountain State has been the first choice among individuals taking part in the Federal Employee Program for many years. Half of West Virginia's federal employees choose Mountain State. Since 1975, thousands of senior citizens have subscribed to one of Mountain State's Medicare supplemental plans. Mountain State also serves the state's coal mining communities, providing coverage to more than 15,000 coal

company employees and their families.

A vision for the future, based on the heritage of the past

Mountain State's vision for the future is seen through the eyes of its president, Gregory K. Smith. Smith was named president in 1995, succeeding Thomas D. Farson, who led the company from 1972 until his 1995 retirement.

"While the company has grown and changed significantly since 1932, we aim to maintain the many unique qualities that set us apart from commercial, out-of-state corporations. We also vow to maintain the lowest possible cost of doing business, in an effort to safeguard our customers' health care dollars," Smith said.

Smith sees the company growing into new markets and developing innovative new products while staying committed to a legacy of ideals. He said the company will continue to nurture its West Virginia roots by tailoring benefit plans to meet community needs.

"We at Mountain State want to remain an integral part of serving West Virginians' health coverage needs by designing health care programs that work for those who need them. As a team of professionals pledged to provide superior service to our customers, we are determined to retain the ideals that made us a Blue Cross and Blue Shield plan."

Mountain State's home office in Parkersburg offers a welcoming environment for customers.

Mountain State Blue Cross & Blue Shield's headquarters building in Parkersburg, the former Union Trust building, is on the National Register of Historic Places.

Profiles in Corpora

TODD A. HANSON

Ashland Inc. in West Virginia

Ashland Exploration explores for and produces oil and natural gas in the United States and overseas. The company's Appalachian basin activities consist primarily of shallow gas development drilling. Ashland Exploration has leaseholds totaling more than 800,000 acres in West Virginia and Kentucky.

In 1924, 33-year-old Paul G. Blazer was hired by Swiss Oil Company of Lexington, Ky., to find a refinery to process Swiss's crude oil production into usable products. Blazer located a 1,000-barrel-per-day facility on the banks of the Big Sandy River in Eastern Kentucky. The refinery stood near the confluence of the Big Sandy and the

mighty Ohio, directly across the Big Sandy from Wayne County, W.Va. Blazer sensed this location, accessible by barge to America's newly emerging industrial heartland, would be propitious for both the short and long term.

Swiss Oil heeded the young entrepreneur's advice, purchased the refinery and installed Paul Blazer as general manager of what became known as Ashland Refining Company, the refining arm of Swiss Oil.

With a handful of employees, Blazer set up offices in three rooms of a bank building in nearby Ashland, Ky. Twenty-five people set about turning the refinery, which had been a money loser, into a profitable enterprise.

From these humble beginnings, Ashland Refining Company eventually grew into Ashland Inc., now a worldwide energy and chemical company.

Ashland Inc. is Kentucky's largest manufacturing corporation and ranks in the top quartile of U.S. firms, based on revenue.

The company employs approximately 31,600 worldwide. The simple, small refinery on the banks of the Big Sandy now boasts crude oil processing capacity of about 213,400 barrels per day and is one of the most sophisticated refineries in the nation.

Employment and refinery production are not the only numbers which have grown. Ashland now serves its customers through six wholly owned operating units and two partially owned coal companies.

Petroleum product marketing

Ashland Petroleum is a leading independent U.S. refiner and a major supplier of petroleum products to West Virginia. The company transports and markets products throughout the Upper Midwest and Central Ohio Valley.

Some 80 percent of the refinery's transportation fuels leave the plant by barge. The river provides economical transportation for refinery products.

Gasoline from Ashland's Catlettsburg, Ky., refinery is marketed in West Virginia under the Ashland, SuperAmerica® and Rich Oil brand names.

SuperAmerica station/stores offer gasoline, fresh-baked goods, automated teller machines, video rentals, automotive accessories and a full range of private-label items.

Known for innovative marketing techniques, some Super-America outlets enhance customer service with integrated point-of-purchase systems and fuel pumps equipped with credit card readers. Others participate in partnerships with leading fast food chains, such as Taco Bell® and Subway.®

Valvoline® brand motor oil is marketed throughout West Virginia, along with Valvoline's Zerex® brand anti-freeze and its Pyroil® Performance Products line of automotive chemicals. Valvoline is among the nation's top five

motor oil marketers, while Zerex is the second leading brand of anti-freeze.

Chemical

Ashland Chemical is the largest distributor of chemicals and solvents in North America. It also occupies preeminent positions in its industrial resins, foundry chemicals, adhesives, water-treatment chemicals, high-purity and other specialty chemicals segments.

Ashland Chemical operates a maleic anhydride plant at Neal in Wayne County, W.Va., that employs 45 individuals.

From 1992 to 1994, Ashland Chemical invested $15 million in the plant to increase production capacity by 30 percent.

Exploration

Ashland Exploration explores for and produces oil and natural gas in the United States and overseas.

SuperAmerica is known for its innovative marketing techniques. To further enhance customer service, some outlets offer fuel pumps equipped with credit card readers.

Some 80 percent of the Catlettsburg refinery's products are transported by barge to distribution centers throughout Ashland's marketing area. There are 15 such locations in West Virginia.

Mingo Logan Coal Co., an independent operating subsidiary of Ashland Coal, has a mine and preparation plant in Mingo County, with nearly 4 million tons of production. Since 1991, Mingo-Logan has added overland conveyors, a computerized preparation plant, storage silos and longwall mining equipment, making it one of the most productive mining complexes in central Appalachia.

The company's U.S. proved reserves total 349 billion cubic feet of natural gas and 900,000 barrels of crude oil, primarily in the Appalachian basin and along the Gulf Coast.

Ashland Exploration's Appalachian basin activities consist primarily of shallow gas development drilling. The company has leaseholds totaling more than 800,000 acres in West Virginia and Kentucky.

The exploration company's Appalachian gas wells provide a dependable base of production near northeastern gas markets.

Ashland Exploration also has nearly 2,650 operating wells in West Virginia and maintains about 1,200 miles of pipeline.

Coal

Long the mainstay of the West Virginia economy, coal is an important part of Ashland Inc. as well.

With highly efficient operations, access to major markets and a strong reserve base in central Appalachia, Ashland's growth-oriented coal investments are positioned to capitalize on improving demand for low-sulfur coal.

Ashland has equity interests in two West Virginia coal companies — Ashland Coal (54 percent) and Arch Mineral Corp. (50 percent).

Ashland Coal is a highly efficient producer and marketer of low-sulfur, central Appalachian steam coal for electric power plants.

Ashland Coal has its headquarters in Huntington, W.Va., and employs nearly 1,400 full-time employees. The coal company produces more than 10 million tons of coal annually.

Hobet Mining, an independent

Ashland Chemical, the largest distributor of chemicals and solvents in North America, operates a maleic anhydride plant at Neal, W.Va. From 1992 to 1994, the company invested $15 million in the plant to increase production capacity.

operating subsidiary, operates mines in Mingo, Logan and Boone counties. Each mine produces in excess of 2 million tons of coal annually.

Mingo-Logan Coal Co., an independent operating subsidiary, has a mine and preparation plant in Mingo County, with nearly 4 million tons of production.

Dal-Tex Coal, an independent operating subsidiary, with operations in Logan County, mines more than 3 million tons of coal annually.

Arch Mineral is a major producer of bituminous coal through its highly efficient operations in West Virginia and three other states.

Arch has a reserve base of roughly 1.6 billion tons of estimated recoverable reserves, with 54 percent of that total consisting of low-sulfur, central Appalachian steam coal.

Arch employs some 810 West Virginia residents. Arch of West Virginia, Catenary Coal and Cumberland River Coal — all independent operating subsidiaries — mine and process coal for steam markets from surface and underground mines in five counties.

A company terminal located south of Kenova, W.Va., near the confluence of the Big Sandy and Ohio rivers, has the capacity to load 6 million tons of coal annually.

Education

From its earliest years, Ashland has been a firm believer in the value of education. Company Founder Paul Blazer came from a family of educators. He set the example for support to education that has endured for more than seven decades.

In recent years, Ashland's support has taken many forms. Since the early 1980s, Ashland's corporate advertising campaign has focused on the importance of quality education.

Ashland also supports education in West Virginia through sponsorship of a variety of scholastic programs, including the Ashland Inc. Foundation, the

Minority Scholarship Program, the Ashland Scholars Program and Ashland Petroleum's Future Engineers Program.

Ashland conducts its Teacher Achievement Awards program in West Virginia as well as a "Day on Campus" student field trip program.

Ashland is an underwriter for WPBY-TV public education television, Mountain Stage and West Virginia Public Radio.

Ashland and West Virginia a continuing partnership

West Virginia has been important to Ashland Inc. since the company was founded in 1924. The Mountain State was among the company's earliest markets, and continues to rely on West Virginia as an important source of energy

reserves and talented employees.

In turn, Ashland and its employees support the communities in which the company operates in numerous civic, cultural and similar endeavors with a goal of giving back to the community some of the benefits Ashland has enjoyed. In addition, both the company and its employees recognize the importance of protecting and maintaining West Virginia's natural beauty and environment.

From its Appalachian roots, Ashland Inc. has grown from a regional refining company into a worldwide energy and chemical company. Ashland and West Virginia appear to be an enduring and mutually beneficial partnership. **Ashland**

Ashland has equity interests in two West Virginia coal companies — Ashland Coal (54 percent) and Arch Mineral Corp. (50 percent). Arch Mineral's Samples Mine in southern West Virginia is fast becoming one of the region's most productive mines. The installation and start-up of a 100-cubic-yard dragline during 1994 doubled the mine's capacity.

Matewan BancShares, Inc.

Matewan BancShares, Inc. is a strong, progressive financial institution strategically positioned to support the planned economic growth of our region resulting from an expanding infrastructure.

The tri-state region served by Matewan BancShares is an area rich in

"Our vision is to be the leading provider of financial services in our region," says Dan R. Moore, President & CEO. "This region is our home and has a lot to offer a company like ours. That's why we are committed to improving the quality of life here through local reinvestment of customer deposits and total support of economic development."

Matewan BancShares is headquartered in Williamson, WV. Its common stock is listed on NASDAQ as "MATE." The company is dedicated to building shareholder wealth, maximizing franchise value and taking the leadership role in innovative banking technology.

natural resources and friendly, hardworking people. It is also a region slated for increased economic development due to an expanding infrastructure, including the construction of highways that will make it more accessible. As part of our planned agenda for growth, Matewan BancShares has quickly become the region's premier financial institution and is poised for the challenges the next decade will bring.

"Our vision is to be the leading provider of financial services in our region," says Dan R. Moore, President & CEO. "This region is our home and has a lot to offer a Company like ours. That's why we are committed to improving the quality of life here through local reinvestment of customer deposits and total support of economic development."

Putting customers first

At Matewan BancShares, we realize that no matter how fast technology advances or how much of it we utilize, our business still revolves around people... our customers, shareholders and employees. We have developed sophisticated systems that enable us to process loans and customer transactions more efficiently, but the end result is customer convenience and fair pricing. Technology must be tempered with the knowledge of customer wants and needs while determining the best method of delivery.

An excellent example of our commitment to practical technology is Express Banking. Matewan BancShares currently has

offices in select Food City supermarkets throughout the region. This modern delivery concept is our Company's way of meeting customers' increasing demands for convenience. Express Banks offer full-service banking seven days a week, and customers can do their banking while they shop for groceries. There's no need to make a separate trip to a more traditional office, unless they so desire.

Matewan Banks' Express Banks are representative of Matewan BancShares' commitment to ValueBanking... exceptional quality and service, always at a fair price.

Bridging the gap between people and technology

Providing a wide array of distribution methods is just one way we put customers first. In addition to extended hours and Express Banking, we give our customers 24-hour access to their accounts. We also supply important information pertaining to account activity, plus lending, investment and savings rates.

In addition, we have a thriving insurance and investment division, Matewan Financial Services, that offers our customers non-traditional bank products such as insurance, mutual funds and annuities.

By keeping pace with advanced banking technology, our customers will soon be able to do their banking at home, at the office, in the car... anywhere around the world.

"For the benefit of our customers, we're committed to keeping pace with technological innovation," says Moore. "We're faster and more accurate today than we were yesterday; we must be even faster and more accurate tomorrow than we are today.

"Customers want absolute control of their money," he explains. "They also want convenience and simplicity." Accordingly, we go the extra mile to bring Matewan Banks to our customers through technology and innovation.

Matewan BancShares is now bringing products and services to

the people of this region that were previously offered only in metropolitan areas by the nation's largest financial institutions.

For example, the lending side of our business is equipped with processing and control systems designed to accommodate lending activities for all Matewan BancShares offices. This technology enables us to drive increased volumes of business at a lower per unit cost.

In spite of Matewan BancShares' bold commitment to keep pace with tomorrow, Moore is quick to add, "No matter what the future brings, Matewan BancShares' mission will remain the same as it has always been... to serve the financial needs of the people and businesses of our region."

The boxed area on the map indicates the region serviced by Matewan BancShares.

West Virginia

Kentucky

Virginia

Inco Alloys International

Inco Alloys International, the alloy manufacturing division of Inco Limited, Canada, is one of the world's leading producers and inventors of nickel-based superalloys. Headquartered in Huntington, the company's alloy products are used worldwide for their resistance to severely corrosive environments and their strength at high temperatures.

These products have traditionally set the standard in the industry. Inco Alloys' success is based on its core philosophy of maintaining the best facilities, the best technology and the best people in the world.

Founded more than 73 years ago, Inco Alloys International has grown to be the largest manufacturing employer in Huntington. Today, the 130-acre production

Inco Alloys International, with its headquarters in Huntington, is the largest facility in the world devoted exclusively to the development, production and sales of nickel-based alloys.

plant in West Virginia is the largest facility of its type in the world devoted exclusively to the development, production, and sale of nickel-base alloys. Inco Alloys also has production facilities in Kentucky, Indiana, North Carolina and Illinois, and sales offices throughout the world.

Decades of growth

Begun as a rolling mill to produce MONEL® alloy, Inco Alloys International, Inc. was first known as Huntington Alloys, Inc. when it began production in May 1922. That year, the plant and its 500 employees began operation and, as a result, the local economy was one million dollars per year

richer. In 1923, the first full year of operation, the plant produced 16 million pounds of six nickel alloy products.

Inco Alloys has grown steadily through the decades. By the 1960s industry's demand for high-nickel alloys led the company to undertake an extensive modernization program. More than $100 million was spent on additional improvements such as the installation of primary mill rolling equipment, two 35-ton electric arc furnaces, an argon oxygen decarburization vessel and a new bar and wire mill. A pilot plant facility in Burnaugh, Kentucky, became a full-fledged production operation with the installation of a 6,000-ton extrusion press and auxiliary equipment for the production of long-length seamless tubing.

Through the addition of sophisticated vacuum arc and vacuum induction melting furnaces, electroslag remelting furnaces and powder metallurgical processes and equipment, the firm has continued to expand the ability of its plants to provide the high-quality material required by an ever more demanding industrial technology.

In 1984, to more accurately reflect its position in a competitive global market, Huntington Alloys, Inc., changed its name to Inco Alloys International, Inc. This followed the consolidation of its rolling mill operations with its sister plant in Hereford, England, under one management headquartered in Huntington with integrated worldwide marketing and sales capabilities.

Today, approximately 1,500 people work at the Huntington and Burnaugh production facilities and more than 3,000 are employed

worldwide. And, Inco Alloys International, Inc. adds more than $115 million per year to the local economy in wages and salaries, local purchases, taxes, benefits and contributions.

Committed to the customer

Employees at Inco Alloys International produce more than 100 precisely controlled alloy compositions, over 75 percent of which were developed in the company's own research laboratories in response to customer needs. The company also offers the finest technical and commercial service for customer support. It has a continuous and substantial investment program in new

The forging press at Inco Alloys International's Huntington operation generates up to 5,000 tons of force. It is one of the largest of its kind in the world.

Steel of West Virginia, Inc.

Steel of West Virginia, Inc. in Huntington, is a compelling success story that is as much a part of the city's history as the railroad, the Ohio River or Marshall University. Steel products have been manufactured at this location since the first decade of this century. The original plant, owned by the Schonthan family, was built in 1907.

The West Virginia Rail Company, as it was known then, was a 60' x 120' wooden structure standing on three acres of real estate and employing fewer than 30 people. The plant today spans 600,000 square feet, stands on 39 acres and employs nearly 600 people.

Steel of West Virginia, Inc. headquarters in Huntington.

fabricate re-bars for use in highway, building and general construction industries.

By 1930 the plant had expanded to 23 acres. The entire plant was rebuilt and the mills were changed from steam-driven to electric-driven motors. By the end of World War II, the plant was known as the largest non-integrated producer of rail steel products in the world.

In 1951, the company purchased additional land increasing the size to 35 acres. In 1952, buildings were erected to house an electric furnace, a blooming mill, and other equipment necessary to produce billets from scrap steel. On October 22, 1952, the first heat of steel was tapped at the new melt shop and the plant was no longer restricted to used rails as a basic raw material. Producing its own billet steel enabled the company to specialize in unique steel shapes

oped a welded mini-beam, a new technology which by 1979 took over the market. This, along with other factors, caused the cost of producing steel at this plant to become noncompetitive. On June 30, 1982, the plant closed.

At a time when the steel industry was not considered a good investment, Bob Bunting, former plant manager of the extinct Connors Steel Plant, along with local investors and a loan from the State of West Virginia purchased the plant for $4.5 million. This marked the beginning of a successful future for the company and its dedicated work force.

Since the rebirth of the plant in August 1982, the company has invested $45 million in modernization projects and state of the art technology. Implementation of new technology enabled the company to once again become a market leader in the truck trailer industry with a rolled mini-beam superior to the welded beam that captured the market in the late 1970's.

Today, the company continues recycling scrap steel to manufacture special steel products for truck trailers, industrial lift trucks, off-highway construction and mining equipment. The plant is able through the use of sophisticated computer-operated equipment to produce hot-rolled steel that formerly had to be fabricated at other facilities.

This vibrant company is a far cry from the small operation owned by the Schonthan family that began with less than 30 employees in a 7,200 square-foot building in the early 20th century. Steel of West Virginia, Inc. is a fresh, innovative company committed to producing the finest quality steel products.

Newly modernized in-line rolling mill.

New auto-stacker equipment.

The original mill was designed to reroll large rail into smaller rail. In 1918, the company installed a second mill designed to split used mainline rail and roll splice bars, re-bars, mine ties, and other shapes. The company increased its operations in 1923 by building a track work accessories manufacturing plant. A steel building was erected to house equipment to

such as sections for major earth moving equipment and lift trucks.

In 1956, the plant became the Connors Steel division of H. K. Porter, a Pittsburgh-based company. By 1964 the product line began to shift to mini-beams used to support the floors of tractor trailer vans. The plant dominated this product line for many years until other manufacturers devel-

Profiles in Excellence Corporate

South Charleston Stamping & Manufacturing, Inc.

United Bankshares, Inc.

Salem-Teikyo University

C.H. Heist Corporation

West Virginia Labor Federation, AFL-CIO

Columbia/HCA Healthcare Corporation

South Charleston Stamping & Manufacturing, Inc.

"**H**ere they come!" exclaims the young boy. "Stop, Mom!" The car quickly comes to a halt as dozens of Canadian geese and their new goslings begin a nightly parade across the busy four-lane highway which runs in front of the South Charleston Stamping & Manufacturing (SCSM) plant.

It's a heartwarming scene as each and every driver, many of them SCSM employees, stop their cars and take the time to care about the safety of the geese families slowly waddling across the highway.

That high level of personal caring—about quality, employee involvement, efficiency, and customer satisfaction—is also readily apparent inside the

Quality Products Pave Path To Growth

A Quality Assurance Program is integrated into every operation and every stage of production at South Charleston Stamping & Manufacturing. Careful and detailed monitoring of each step in the work flow leads to the ultimate level of customer satisfaction. Not only are buyer's exact specifica-

hangs in the SCSM office, too.

The very prestigious ISO 9000 certification has been earned by SCSM, the first American sheet metal stamping facility to receive this designation.

Dedication to quality has created a loyal customer roster. General Motors is SCSM's principle buyer. Stampings are also produced for Toyota, Ford, Saturn,

immense building where South Charleston Stamping & Manufacturing produces automotive sheet metal stampings for the worldwide market. Numerous prestigious awards have been won for consistent adherence to the highest standards, not only by SCSM but also by its president, John T. Wise.

tions met, but SCSM's own rigid Quality Assurance Program criteria are reached.

In 1991, SCSM received General Motors' "Mark of Excellence" award. GM again recognized outstanding workmanship through presenting South Charleston Stamping & Manufacturing with the 1993 QSP Award as Outstanding Sheet Metal Supplier Worldwide. The Ford 101 recognition and a perfect rating from Saturn have been earned. Chrysler's Quality of Excellence Award

and Freightliner.

A new customer, preparing to introduce an innovative product to the U.S. and international markets, has recently recognized SCSM's excellence with a long-term contract. Mercedes-Benz plans to introduce its all-activity vehicle in 1997 and a large portion of the sheet metal stampings are to be produced at SCSM. Mercedes' highest standards will be assured through the workmanship already established at South Charleston, coupled with the partnership that

state has allowed it to become one of West Virginia's chief proponents.

"Our growth will continue as the growth of the state continues. We are committed to helping the state prosper economically and socially. Our commitment does not end at providing capital for investment and supporting business; we also have to take an active part in the state and the communities in which we are located to help make them better places to live and work," Adams said.

That legacy of active participation has been a part of United's heritage since its inception, and continues today.

Perhaps nowhere is West Virginia's belief in itself seen more than in its support of West Virginia University. United has helped increase that support as corporate sponsor of WVU athletics since 1990, and is a major contributor to the WVU Foundation.

"Our sponsorship of the WVU athletic programs is just one way we show our support for the state. All of our individual offices take an active role in their communities, with employees serving on boards and committees, sponsoring local events and helping to make a difference in their communities," Adams said.

As a company that has been blessed in many ways, United believes in giving back to the communities it serves. In 1995, United contributed over $500,000 to such organizations as the United Way, the YWCA, the Salvation Army, the West Virginia Business Roundtable, W.V. Kids Count and many more. United paid approximately $4 million in state and local taxes and over $12 million in federal taxes. United is a company that is dedicated to serving.

With all of its dedication to the state and community, United remains committed to customer service. As the challenge to be the best grows, so does United's commitment to its customers, providing the best services, accounts and unparalleled employees. Whether a mortgage for a new home, a consumer loan for a new car or to help with a college education, a commercial loan for a business or one of United's many checking and savings accounts, investments in CDs or Money Market accounts, trust services or a United Master Card or Visa, United has the right tools to help its customers meet their individual needs.

"As we approach the 21st Century, the challenges we face continue to grow. We at United will always be committed to our mission of excellence in service for our shareholders, for our customers, for our employees and for the communities we serve," Adams said. "We are proud to be known as 'West Virginia's Bank.'"

Richard M. Adams,
Chairman of the Board
and Chief Executive Officer
United Bankshares, Inc.

Salem-Teikyo University

Founded in 1888, century-old Salem College merged with Teikyo University of Tokyo, Japan, in July 1989, to create the first international center of its kind in the United States.

With a unique modular calendar and a global mission, Salem-Teikyo University is

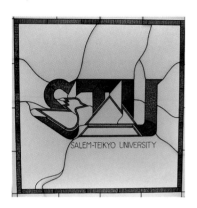

"Not only is history being made in West Virginia, but it is a day in which history is being made in American higher education." — Ronald E. Ohl, President Salem-Teikyo University

different from any other campus in the world. The mission of the university is to educate the world citizen who is able to make decisions from an international point of view without prejudice.

The modular calendar allows for a great deal of flexibility in scheduling courses, and enables students to focus their talent, energy, and creativity on one course at a time. Salem-Teikyo operates on a 12 modular calendar. A module consists of 18 class days normally followed by a two-day break. Within a module, students attend the same class each weekday for at least four hours per day.

Another advantage of the modular calendar is that students may register for classes at the beginning of any module, thus it is possible to enter college at times other than the traditional fall or spring semesters. Students must

enroll in at least six modules (24 credit hours) to be considered a full time student.

Salem-Teikyo students are engaged in an intense learning experience where scholarship is highly valued and where every aspect of the college experience includes an international dimension. Classes become an exchange of ideas between ambassadors from all over the world. Students have the opportunity to understand and appreciate how someone from another culture might view the same situation quite differently. At Salem-Teikyo, learning extends beyond the traditional walls of the classroom to the world.

Salem-Teikyo seeks to educate world citizens - men and women who take responsibility for their own education while gaining the knowledge and self-confidence to achieve leadership roles in their home countries and in the global

arena. As a part of this mission, Salem-Teikyo provides opportunities for study abroad and international internships in the Netherlands, the reunited Germany and Japan. Each of the programs includes field trips to help immerse the participants into the culture in which they are living for that period of time. Home stays with a host family are frequently part of the study abroad experience.

Students at Salem-Teikyo live, laugh, and learn in an environment respectful of individual differences. Athletics and personal fitness activities also contribute to students' educational experiences. Salem-Teikyo intercollegiate programs field a variety of teams: men and women's basketball, tennis and swimming; men's baseball, soccer, rugby and golf; women's softball and volleyball; and coed cheerleading and equestrian events.

Salem-Teikyo University prepares a richly diverse student body to lead the world of tomorrow.

C.H. HEIST Corp.

C. H. Heist Corp. has enjoyed a long partnership with West Virginia and her industrial community. The Company was incorporated in Buffalo, New York, in 1949 in the business of applying protective coatings to a wide range of industrial sites. By 1954 the company had expanded into the Ohio Valley and was

actively quoting on painting and sandblasting projects in both Parkersburg and Charleston.

In 1954 the company was awarded the annual painting contract at the Union Carbide Institute plant and C. H. Heist Corp. officially became a part of the West Virginia business community. The following year the company was awarded the painting contract at the Union Carbide South Charleston facility. This was a major milestone for the company because it launched us into a new business upon which we would base our growth and success for decades to come.

Because some areas of the plant were considered explosive environments, abrasive blasting was prohibited. As a result Union Carbide wrote into its specifications "hydroblasting" as the means

for surface preparation. C. H.Heist Corp. bought two industrial pumps, adapted the fluid blocks for high pressure service and the "hydroblasting" industry was born. The early units could generate up to 4,000 PSI at 40 gallons per minute.

We quickly discovered that

besides surface preparation for painting, high pressure water cleaning was ideal for cleaning process piping, sewers, and a wide range of process equipment. By the mid 1960's we increased operating pressures to 10,000 PSI. And by the mid-1970's available pressures were increased to 20,000 PSI. Today C. H. Heist Corp. supplies hydroblasting equipment that ranges up to 36,000 PSI from its twenty-six locations in the United States and Canada. In addition to sandblasting, painting, and hydroblasting, the company also offers wet and dry vacuum, insulation, field repair, and turnaround services

At Heist we take pride in the kind of service we provide for our clients: prompt, courteous, knowledgeable, and highly skilled. We know that service is our business. Who delivers that service? People. And people who deliver the best service are full-time, year-round employees who are motivated to work and possess strong company loyalty. These qualities are what Heist people are all about, and nowhere in our organization is there a

stronger group than our employees from West Virginia.

In West Virginia we have enjoyed long-term relationships with many of the industrial sites located along the Ohio and Kanawha rivers. We have such relationships with E. I. DuPont's Washington Works, and Belle West Virginia plants; Union Carbide's Institute, South Charleston, and Tech Center sites; Rhone-Poulenc AG; Arco Chemicals; Flexsys; FMC Corporation; Aristech Chemicals; Clearon Corporation; and American Electric Power.

Today through a focused partnering effort Heist has become a permanent part of the day-to-day functions of many Fortune 500 companies. In many of these companies' plants, Heist commits a number of employees, trucks and pieces of equipment to stay on site permanently. We participate in management planning sessions, so we can respond immediately with additional labor and equipment during peak production times and plant outages.

C. H. Heist Corp. is a public company listed on the American Stock Exchange (HST).

West Virginia Labor Federation, AFL-CIO

West Virginia labor history is American history. In 1863, when the Northwestern counties of Virginia became a state, the new state of West Virginia adopted the motto, "Mountaineers are Always Free." This declaration makes it fitting that our state has been the site of many struggles for workers' rights:

* In August 1921, miners, during their effort to unionize the Southern coal fields, were attacked at Blair Mountain by state national guardsmen and federal troops. This four-day battle was the only time in American history, to date, that the federal government has bombed its own citizens.

* One of the nation's very first successful steel mill organizing drives took place at Inco Alloys in Huntington during the Great Depression. These campaigns saw the use of the sit-down strike as an organizing tool. Although automobile workers in Flint, Michigan, can claim the nation's most famous sit-down strikes, sit-downs in West Virginia preceded those in Flint.

Headquarters of the West Virginia Federation of Labor, AFL-CIO, located at 501 Broad Street, Charleston

* Farmington, West Virginia, was the site of a 1968 explosion that killed 78 miners. Less than a year later, in 1969, Congress enacted the first national mine health and safety law.

* The Ravenswood Aluminum Company lockout of Steelworkers in the early 1990's was a key factor in focusing national attention on the use of strikebreakers. Congressional debate on this issue has been heated, and continues through 1995.

As history shows, the fight for freedom in America — for social and economic justice — has frequently found its roots in West Virginia. Mountaineers, it seems, if not always free, have never turned away from pursuing their freedom.

In unity, there is progress

From 1937 through 1955, the national House of Labor was a house divided. Because of differing strategies and priorities, craft and industrial unions were split between two separate organizations, the American Federation of Labor (A.F. of L.) and the Congress of Industrial Organizations (C.I.O.). However, West Virginia unions maintained the spirit of goodwill and solidarity.

On November 22, 1957, the West Virginia Labor Federation officially merged in the very same city, Huntington, where the first state labor body was born in 1903. This meant an end to an artificial split in state organized labor. For the years prior to the official reunion, West Virginia unions cooperated with each other often, particularly on political and legislative issues.

The first Constitutional Convention of the West Virginia Labor Federation, AFL-CIO, elected Miles C. Stanley, a Steelworker from Local Union 3715 of Dunbar, as its first President. The new organization counted a membership of more than 60,000 in 363 local unions. This, in a state where the 1957 unemployment rate topped 18%. The AFL-CIO State headquarters at 1624 Kanawha Boulevard, Charleston, had much to do and was a very busy place.

With West Virginia labor's unity, came the fierce determination to confront the many problems facing the state. State towns and counties were as underdeveloped as any of the emerging nations of the world. Poverty, children with fragile health, inadequate and dangerous infrastructure, and poor education were issues faced by West Virginians. Officers and delegates at the First Constitutional Convention spoke of the great urgency to confront these crises. The Federation advocated a better economic, political and social climate so that "all men, irrespective of race, color, creed or nationality can have a more abundant and free life."

Early on, the importance of education was recognized as a method for promoting effective leadership among union activists. To make this understanding a reality, the state AFL-CIO, with West Virginia University, organized the Labor Extension Service in 1958. "Summer School," as it has been known for 37 years, is a week-long program of general discussions and instruction designed to help solve problems encountered within a local union. Students attend classes on leadership, government and politics, union administration, grievance procedures, and the latest changes in state and federal labor law.

Activism & altruism

Nineteen-Sixty was a politically significant year for the nation and for West Virginia. The frightening condition of Appalachia was finally emerging as an important national issue; the civil rights movement was growing in intensity and scope. Organized labor, too, took some action of its own on civil rights. The 1960 Constitutional Convention was to be held at the old Daniel Boone Hotel in Charleston. Curiously, however, a room for an African-American delegate "could not be found." Learning this, the Federation threatened to move the entire convention from the hotel. Not wanting to lose the Convention, the hotel was suddenly able to "find" a room for the delegate.

Following his election in 1960, President John F. Kennedy worked to address state problems and those of the Appalachian region. Following Kennedy's assassination in 1963, President Lyndon Johnson began constructing his vision for the nation, The Great Society. Great Society programs focused even greater attention on improving conditions in Appalachia. One program, The Appalachian Council — headquartered in Charleston — is a job training program that is, in 1995, still providing individuals with workplace skills. More than merely making skill training available to those who find it, Appalachian Council programs recruit underprivileged individuals from hollows and cities to gain the competencies necessary to earn a living — all to build more stable and prosperous communities.

Strong community spirit and commitment has always been a priority, and that altruism continues today. Officers, staff, regional labor councils, local unions, and members have contributed countless hours to the needs of state residents. Disaster recovery, blood banks, food banks, construction for nonprofit and civic projects, Scouting, coaching, and in endless other roles, union members have always been there for others.

In keeping with its mission to improve lives, the Federation in 1967, established the Human Resource Development Foundation, Inc. (HRDF) and the Human Resource Development and Employment, Inc. (HRDE). HRDF provides adult basic education and occupational training to the unemployed and economically disadvantaged. These programs over the years have put thousands of West Virginians to work, paying taxes, and contributing to the state's economy.

HRDE, working in concert with Housing and Urban Development, has constructed 10 facilities across the state since 1971 to meet the housing needs of retirees, low-income families and the disabled. Within these structures are 712 units offering efficiencies, one- and two-bedroom quarters. In 1993, HRDE expanded the scope of its services and opened Unity Hospice Care, Inc. Hospice Care brings badly needed health care to residents in Lewis, Braxton, Gilmer and Upshur counties.

As it has done for nearly 40 years AFL-CIO Community Services, currently under the direction of Federation Secretary-Treasurer Jack McComas, constantly seeks to serve its fellow citizens.

New leadership, old issues

In May 1974, following the death of Miles Stanley, Joseph W. Powell was elected as President. Powell, then the AFL-CIO COPE Director, previously had served in various leadership roles for unions. Also in 1974, operations were moved to Boulevard Towers at 1018 Kanawha Boulevard. New headquarters did not change the fact that working people struggled against many of the same old foes. Without the foundations of political action, legislative work and organizing support, the Federation's effectiveness would be greatly diminished. Labor is proud that legislative accomplishments have benefitted all working people — union and nonunion. Victories in increasing unemployment compensation benefits, creating a more accessible and open government at all levels, advocating a state minimum wage, improving the infrastructure, workplace safety and fairness, better conditions, wages and benefits for state employees, and election law reform have contributed to our state becoming a more attractive place to do business and raise a family.

This ever-growing activity necessitated yet another decision regarding location. The AFL-CIO purchased property at 501 Broad

Street, Charleston, for the building of a unity center. The project, completed in 1981, is a modern three-story structure. On the building is a brass plate that reads, *The Stanley Building*, named for the Federation's first president.

The goals of the AFL-CIO remain fundamental: a living wage, health benefits, and workplace safety for all. West Virginia has the resources to make our state an even better place in which to invest and reside. The Wall Street Journal has noted that our people offer prospective employers a workforce second to none — a workforce that is the backbone and the engine of our economy. As Abraham Lincoln observed in 1863, "Labor is prior to, and independent of capital. Capital is only the fruit of labor and could never have existed if labor had not first existed."

The West Virginia Federation of Labor believes all who contribute to our state's progress should share in its prosperity. For all our citizens, especially for our children and their future, it is the right thing to do.

The Morgantown Unity Manor in Morgantown, West Virginia. Unity Manor is one of 10 housing facilities operated by the Human Resource Development and Employment, Inc., a subsidiary of the West Virginia AFL-CIO.

Columbia/HCA Healthcare Corporation

Columbia/HCA Healthcare Corporation is the nation's largest health care services provider, owning and operating 340 hospital and 125 outpatient surgery centers and other health care facilities. With approximately 62,000 licensed beds in 36 states, England and Switzerland, employing over 260,000 people, Columbia is the nation's tenth-largest employer.

History

Columbia/HCA Healthcare Corporation was created in February 1994 when Columbia Healthcare Corporation and Healthcare Corporation of America merged, and grew substantially larger in March of 1995, with the merger of HealthTrust, Inc.

Columbia Healthcare Corporation was created in September 1993 with the merger of Columbia Hospital Corporation of Fort Worth, Texas and Galen Health Care of Louisville, Kentucky. The Columbia-Galen merger created a company with 95 hospitals in 18 states.

Healthcare Corporation of America was founded in 1968 in Nashville, Tennessee, by Thomas Frist Sr., M.D., and his son, Thomas Frist, Jr., M.D. and the late Jack Massey. The company went public in 1969 and grew rapidly through a series of acquisitions and management contracts. In 1988, during a period of restructuring, management and outside investors purchased the company in a leveraged buy out. Then in 1992, responding to changes in the industry and stock market, HCA sold 34 million shares of common stock, again becoming a publicly traded company. Prior to the Columbia merger, HCA had 96 hospitals in 21 states.

HealthTrust, Inc. was formed in a leveraged buyout of 104 Hospital Corporation of America hospitals in 1987. In May 1994, HealthTrust acquired EPIC Healthcare Group, which owned and operated 34 hospitals in 10 states and provided certain specialty services including home health care, rehabilitation services and health care management services.

Strategy implementation

Columbia is building comprehensive networks of health care services in local markets, integrating various services to deliver patient care with maximum efficiency. The strategy includes streamlining operations, sharing high-technology equipment and personnel where appropriate, and using economies of scale when contracting for medical supplies and administrative services.

Columbia has significantly broadened the range of services provided as evidenced by the new psychiatric units, rehabilitation units, skilled nursing units and home health agencies. In addition, Columbia has expanded its capabilities to create and manage physician practices to further coordinate physician services with provider networks.

In an effort to reduce the cost of providing services, many hospital supply purchases were converted to national contracts which were negotiated in connection with Columbia's enhanced purchasing power, and through numerous hospital consolidations which eliminated the high fixed costs of one facility while spreading the remaining fixed costs of the other facility over a larger patient base.

While adding new services and working to reduce costs, Columbia also has focused on continually improving the quality of care and services provided. Columbia is also aggressively implementing clinical information systems in each hospital. These systems, which provide real-time access of patient medical record data to physicians at home and in their offices, allow the medical staffs to better manage patient conditions and react accordingly.

Through these strategies, Columbia/HCA expects to become the model for health care delivery not only in the United States, but worldwide.

Greenbrier Valley Medical Center

Offering a wide range of general and specialized services, Greenbrier Valley Medical Center is a 122-bed facility located in Fairlea, just outside of Lewisburg.

The dedicated staff at Greenbrier Valley Medical Center makes every effort to provide the kind of attentive service that helps promote patient progress and recovery. Accredited by JCAHO, the hospital strives to meet the needs of the community.

In April 1995, the Emergency Department underwent renovations and was expanded by approximately 700%, from 950 square feet to 6,520 square feet to include obstetric, pediatric, orthopedic, trauma, and ENT rooms.

Putnam General Hospital

Putnam General Hospital, located in Hurricane, is a 68-bed medical and surgical facility. Since opening in 1983, the hospital's medical staff has grown to include more than 150 physicians, practicing in more than 25 areas of specialization.

Accredited by JCAHO, the hospital offers intensive care and telemetry units, and a fully equipped inpatient and outpatient

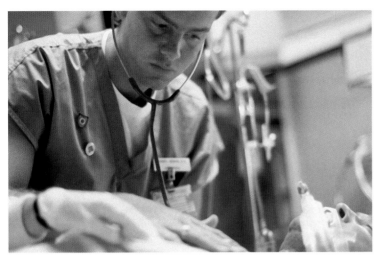

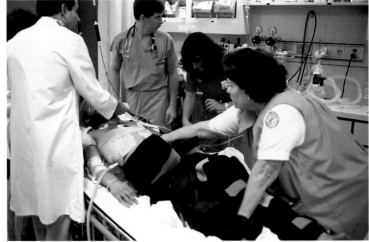

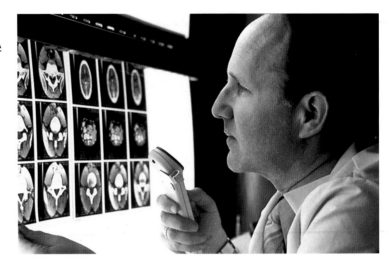

⬦ COLUMBIA/HCA
Healthcare Corporation

surgery department and a state-of-the-art radiology department.

In 1995, the hospital underwent a significant expansion including the addition of an Emergency Fast Track, and the Putnam Rehab Center.

Putnam General Hospital also has two satellite facilities, Putnam Primary Care Center and Doctors Park Clinic.

River Park Hospital

Located in Huntington, River Park Hospital is the largest free-standing psychiatric hospital in the state.

The 165-bed hospital offers a full range of programs, including 24-hour assessment and referral services, inpatient and partial hospitalization programming and outpatient services for children, adolescents, adults and families.

To enhance the establishment of healthy routines and relationship building, patients use the hospital's outdoor walking trail, fitness stations, gymnasium and lounge areas which are integrated into the daily activities therapy.

River Park is accredited by JCAHO and is a member of the National Association of Psychiatric Hospitals.

Raleigh General Hospital,

Raleigh General Hospital, founded in 1922, is a 275-bed general acute care facility located in Beckley and is accredited by JCAHO.

With a medical staff of approximately 170 physicians, the hospital offers to the residents of southern West Virginia a broad range of services ranging from emergency medicine, with a level III trauma center, to general surgery. The hospital is the sole provider of inpatient obstetrical care in Raleigh County and offers pediatric and newborn services, Level III neonatal, and intensive care. It is also the sole provider of cardiac catherization services in the area.

Saint Francis Hospital

Saint Francis Hospital in Charleston, established in 1913, is a 200-bed acute care facility with more than 290 medical staff members including primary care and specialty physicians. Fully accredited by the JCAHO, Saint Francis Hospital provides specialized treatment programs including Acute Care 24 for those requiring immediate medical assistance,

Center for Pain Relief, Cancer Treatment, Skilled Nursing Unit, Healthscope, a primary care center, and One-Day Surgery Center.

St. Luke's Hospital

Located in Bluefield, St. Luke's Hospital, a 79-bed acute care, medical-surgical facility has provided health care services since its organization in 1904. St. Luke's is fully accredited by JCAHO and received their highest rating of Accreditation with Commendation in the last two consecutive surveys.

With approximately 95 physicians on staff, the modern facility, completed in 1982, provides a state-of-the-art Emergency department and Surgical services including laser and outpatient procedures as well as Pain Management and Industrial Medicine programs.

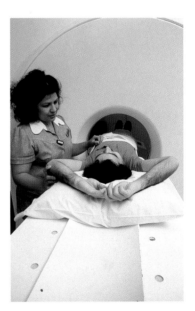

Profiles in Corporate Excellence

The Greenbrier

CNG Transmission Corporation

American Concrete Pavement Association - Northeast Chapter

Acordia of West Virginia

The Neighborgall Construction Company

Charleston Area Medical Center, Inc.

The Greenbrier

I f it's true that first impressions last a lifetime, then there is no question why The Greenbrier has been regarded as America's Resort for more than two centuries. Since its founding as a "place of healing and rejuvenating mineral waters" in 1778, The Greenbrier has made indelible first impressions on guests from every walk of

life; from U.S. presidents and heads of state; to celebrities and captains of industry to generations of American families who return year after year to find relaxation and recreation in this magnificent Allegheny Mountains upland valley of West Virginia.

Although there is a compelling comfortable timelessness reflected throughout this 6,500-acre estate, guests are quick to sense the resort's commitment of "The Greenbrier is ladies and gentlemen being served by ladies and gentlemen."® Instead of standing on its illustrious history and significant laurels, The Greenbrier,

nestled in a seemingly endless scenic mountain landscape, is dedicated to being in the vanguard of providing an environment and amenities that appeal to the ever changing lifestyles of its guests.

In the beginning, The Greenbrier appealed to those seeking the rebirth of body and spirit that was the embodiment of the promise of the natural mineral spring waters. Although today's resort offers a myriad of other "refreshments for both body and mind," the site of the original spring is faithfully preserved in a Spring House that dates back to the early 1800s. Visitors to the Spring House, today

may still partake of the water while relaxing in the marble-column domed rotunda glistening in the afternoon sun. Atop the dome is a statue of the Greek goddess of youth, Hebe, a fitting icon to what is represented by the site, itself.

Throughout its early history, the lure and legend of the resort grew to truly epitomize the literal meaning of "resort," as "a place to go for rest and relaxation, a pleasant escape from the demands of the daily cares."

The mountains surrounding The Greenbrier form a natural tapestry that provides a unique and enchanting location that guests

Ted J. Kleisner, President and Managing Director

North Entrance

throughout the years have found to be all that the word "resort" is defined to offer.

As great an appeal as the natural beauty of the estate has been to guests throughout the generations, The Greenbrier owes considerable homage to the beauty of Southern Belles who adopted it as their own "playground of gentility" in the years immediately after the American Civil War, or the War Between the States, as many Southern families chose to call it at that time.

Debuts, elegant balls, gallops, cotillions and other dazzling social events became commonplace at The Greenbrier. And the management and staff of the resort reemphasized their commitment to service that still is a part of the living tradition at the resort. While the season of 1869 was long remembered for the galaxy of prominent Americans who gathered at White Sulphur Springs, that summer another event occurred which profoundly altered the course of the resort's history.

On June 29, the first passenger train over the newly laid tracks of the Chesapeake and Ohio Railway reached the resort. The arrival of that train, carrying railroad magnate Collis P. Huntington among its passengers, was a triumphant day for The Greenbrier, helping insure its very survival because the resort could boast of service directly to its main gate.

The iron wheels drawn by steaming locomotives made The Greenbrier an accessible and natural destination for travelers from both North and South, and made possible the enduring nature of the resort.

Since that day more than 125 years ago, the railroad has played a major part in the life of the resort, and today CSX Corporation, the successor to the C&O, owns and operates The Greenbrier with impeccable standards of service and amenities.

The Spring House.

In the last 10 years The Greenbrier has invested more than $100 million into redecorating and refurbishing the resort as well as adding to its diverse offerings of programs, recreation and relaxation designed to provide a unique experience to its tens of thousands of guests every year.

Architecturally delightful, and a feast for the eyes, The Greenbrier maintains more than 672 guest rooms, suites, guest houses and estate houses the year 'round for the comfort and convenience of its social and business visitors and families who keep returning to the resort season after season.

Many families have been making The Greenbrier their "place of reunion" for generations, while still others are discovering The Greenbrier for the first time.

Some of the guest houses date back to the mid 1800's, although their accommodations are impeccably maintained and refurbished to reflect the needs and lifestyles of today's families and other guests.

Of course, The Greenbrier Spa and Mineral Baths offers guests the ultimate in spa facilities and treatments throughout the year and carries on the tradition of the original "healing mineral waters" that was the founding hallmark of the resort.

Scotch sprays and swiss showers, facial and full body

massages and treatments, steaming whirlpool baths and sauna rooms all are part of The Greenbrier Spa, complemented by a full service beauty salon with hair styling, manicures and pedicures round out a program of cosmetic revitalization.

Paramount among recreational activities is championship golf on the resort's three 18-hole courses, each beginning and ending at the Golf Club. Designed by world-renowned golf course architects, each of the three courses offers its own unique challenges and excitement.

The Greenbrier Course, originally designed by George O'Neil, completed in 1924 and redesigned by Jack Nicklaus in 1977, is the only golf course in the world to host both the prestigious international Ryder Cup and Solheim Cup Matches. The United States team in each instance, the Ryder Cup in 1979 and the Solheim Cup in 1994, won the matches.

In addition to the attractiveness of the game and the courses, golf at The Greenbrier also can boast of having one of the game's greatest legends, Slammin' Sam Snead, as the resort's golf professional emeritus. The winner of more tournaments than any other professional golfer (84) Sam also holds the record for posting a score of 59 on the original Greenbrier Course in 1959 playing in a tournament named for him, the Sam Snead Spring Festival. That tournament is still played annually at the resort, attracting top professional and amateur players from throughout the nation.

The prominence of golf at The Greenbrier has grown consistent with the sport itself, and today players from throughout the world look forward to coming here and challenging these wonderfully landscaped and maintained courses.

Among other timeless popular recreational activities still offered today at The Greenbrier are tennis, horseback riding, croquet, swimming, fishing and a gun club. Tennis facilities include 15 outdoor and five indoor courts as well as a complete tennis club house and pro shop.

#2 on the Greenbrier course.

Profiles in Corporate Excellence

Vecellio & Grogan, Inc.

Marshall University

Robert C. Byrd Institute for Advanced Flexible Manufacturing

Banc One West Virginia Corporation

West Virginia Paving

Highland Hospital

Vecellio & Grogan, Inc.

Leo Vecellio believed he was born to build roads. He was born October 16, 1915, and as a 5-year-old played under his parents' house with his friend, Frank Hatfield, building roads. So deep were the cuts the boys made around the foundation blocks that Leo's father, Enrico, had to remind him not to dig near the blocks

or the house would collapse.

Born January 14, 1878, in Auronzo, Italy, and trained as a stonemason in Switzerland, Enrico came to America in 1900 to erect coke ovens. With two helpers, he could finish an oven in a 14-hour day, earning $75 for the job. Returning to Italy to build his parents a home, Enrico married Anna Maria Del Favero on September 6, 1909, and they set

Enrico Vecellio, 1878-1954

sail for America on their wedding day. Again building coke ovens, he intended to return to Italy after saving some money. However, his hard work, honesty and respect for people who depended on his word established the giant business that today is Vecellio & Grogan, Inc.

Enrico built many coke ovens and, later, railroad beds and coal roads, for the Norfolk & Western Railroad. Moving often, he built many public and coal-company roads. He first worked alone, then in partnership with his cousin Arthur Zande beginning in 1916, and with the Waugh Brothers in 1921. In 1923, he established a partnership which included his

respected shovel operator, Littleton Coleman, and named it Gilbert Construction, after the community that had treated the Vecellios so well. In 1928, the company incorporated and included a third shareholder, Richard B. Gay.

The company's mules and wagons soon gave way to trucks, and in the early 1930s, diesel dozers and shovels were added. Gilbert Construction expanded rapidly, and the three men began individually managing in three areas of West Virginia. Beginning a new project on Route 19, the Midland Trail, in 1931, Enrico moved permanently to Beckley. Erma Vecellio had finished business school in 1930 and joined the company to manage the office. Shortly thereafter, Enrico hired a hard-working and knowledgeable man, Eugene Grogan. Erma and Gene were married December 29, 1933.

At age 10, Leo began working for the company during the summers and by the time he entered Virginia Polytechnic Institute to study civil engineering, he was experienced in every aspect of road construction. Graduating in 1938, he realized his boyhood dreams when he and Gene Grogan established the partnership of Vecellio & Grogan, which also included Enrico. V&G received an award to build a five-mile section of road from Man to Verner, followed in 1941 by a large coal-site preparation project. Just before Leo entered the Army in 1942, V&G received a large award to construct an airport runway at Cumberland, Maryland. Leo hired Norman Trevillion to assist Enrico and Gene Grogan in his absence.

Leo returned to civilian life in

1945. Just prior to his discharge, he met Evelyn Pais of Keystone and they married that December 29. Their first son, Leo Jr., was born October 26, 1946; a second son, Ricky, on January 23, 1953; then a daughter, Patricia, on November 17, 1958.

V&G prospered under Trevillion's management during the war and many jobs were joint-ventured with Gilbert Construction. Once back in Leo's hands, V&G expanded into coal mining at Grundy, Virginia. Enrico hated strip mining because it destroyed the environment, especially trees. However, if Enrico had lived into the 1970s he would have been proud of his son's leadership in establishing mining regulations and land reclamation.

By the late 1940s, Enrico had retired but was always at Leo Sr.'s side to provide well-seasoned knowledge concerning projects. Then, on March 26, 1954, Enrico died, leaving Leo Sr. alone at the helm.

Both coal and construction returned reasonable profits into the early 1950s when coal prices dropped and construction jobs were scarce. However, the development of Flat Top Lake in 1951 helped shore up the job inventory.

Coal continued to play a role in Leo Sr.'s life. In 1953, Southern Coals was established, followed by Ranger Fuel Corp. in 1960, then Sterling Smokeless Coals. Southern Coals continued to mine coal until 1963 and then functioned as a grading company until 1967 when it was merged with V&G. In 1970, Ranger was sold to Pittston and Sterling to Eastern Associated Coal Co.

Profiles in Corporate Excellence

West Virginia University

SEM Partners, Inc.

One Valley Bank

Thomas Memorial Hospital

Pocahontas Land Corporation

American Electric Power

GERALD S. RATLIFF

West Virginia University

A land-grant institution established in 1867, West Virginia University today comprises 14 colleges and schools and offers 164 degree programs from the bachelor's through the doctoral and first-professional levels. Undergraduate programs range from aerospace engineering to theatre, from medical technology to

recreation and parks management, from landscape architecture to speech pathology and audiology.

The university also offers a highly competitive master's degree program in physical therapy — the only accredited program in the state — a redesigned nursing curriculum, a top-notch engineering program and the state's only accredited College of Business and Economics. A wide range of health science programs are taught at the Robert C. Byrd Health Sciences Center through Schools of Medicine, Dentistry, Nursing and Pharmacy, and WVU is home to the state's only law school. WVU has also introduced a ground-breaking five-year, dual-degree program to educate future teachers. The university's global connection is demonstrated in its World Music Center in the College of Creative Arts. Students cross geographic and cultural boundaries with instruments from Indonesia, China, Japan and other countries, including one of the world's largest collections of African instruments.

The university's programs attract students from all of West Virginia's 55 counties, 48 other states, the District of Columbia,

A WVU landmark, Woodburn Hall, provides the backdrop for this student-led tour.

Puerto Rico, the Virgin Islands and 76 other nations. Fall 1995 enrollment was 21,517.

WVU is accredited by the North Central Association of Colleges and Schools, and is designated a Research I University by the Carnegie Foundation for the Advancement of Teaching.

Main campus

Located in Morgantown among the mountains of northern West Virginia near the intersection of I-79 and I-68, WVU is within easy traveling distance of the metropolitan areas of Pittsburgh, about 70 miles north, and Baltimore and Washington, D.C., about 200 miles to the east. Morgantown itself is a comfortably sized community of about 26,000.

The main Morgantown campus actually consists of three

distinct campuses — Downtown, Evansdale and the Robert C. Byrd Health Sciences Center. The Personal Rapid Transit (PRT) system has been shuttling people among the campuses since the U.S. Department of Transportation built it more than 20 years ago. PRT cars are computer directed and electric-powered; they zip along a concrete and steel guideway.

Altogether, the three campuses contain 158 buildings on 673 acres. Facilities range from the stately 19th century structures of Woodburn Circle to gleaming high-tech facilities devoted to research.

Not all WVU students are in Morgantown. University regional campuses include the Charleston Division of the WVU Health Sciences Center, the Wheeling Division of the School of Medi-

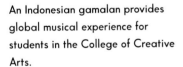

An Indonesian gamalan provides global musical experience for students in the College of Creative Arts.

At WVU, teaching means intellectual collaboration. Creative writing professor and author Gail Adams chats with her students.

WVU's 25th Rhodes Scholar Carolyn Conner at the Mountainlair, a building devoted to enhancing the student experience.

cine, Potomac State College in Keyser, WVU-Parkersburg, the WVU Institute of Technology in Montgomery and six off-campus graduate centers.

Additionally, satellite technology beams WVU to sites around the state and reaches students who could not otherwise attend the university.

Exceptional faculty and students

West Virginia University is making a difference in people's lives through education, discovery and outreach.

Educating students is the university's top priority, and teaching means much more than lecturing. WVU faculty involve students through hands-on research, the newest technology, foreign exchanges, service learning projects and innovative programs. Students emerge from WVU with a broad liberal arts education and preparation for successful careers.

WVU is more a convergence of talented people than a collection of buildings. In particular, the university takes pride in its faculty, many of whom have chosen the institution as their permanent home for scholarship. More than 85 percent of WVU's full-time teaching faculty have earned doctorates or the highest degree

offered in their disciplines. Many are nationally and internationally recognized experts in their fields. More than 70 percent of the university's classes are taught by full-time faculty — surpassing the national average for state colleges and universities.

Recognition has come to teachers who excel. Through 1995-96, the Carnegie Foundation for the Advancement of Teaching had honored eight WVU faculty as West Virginia Professor of the Year and university faculty had received one gold and two silver national awards. Five WVU faculty have been named Professor of the Year by the West Virginia Faculty Merit Foundation, and university faculty consistently win Fulbright grants that provide teaching and research opportunities around the world.

WVU's undergraduate student-faculty ratio is 17:1.

The work of outstanding teachers is reflected in students' accomplishments. By 1996, WVU had produced 25 Rhodes scholars, 15 Goldwater scholars and in the fall of that year, the Truman Scholarship Foundation awarded the university a medallion in recognition of its exceptional record of 13 Truman scholars.

More than 60 percent of WVU students receive some sort of scholarship or other form of

financial aid, totaling more than $80 million annually.

Once they arrive on campus, students are both nurtured and challenged.

The university's Honors Program involves about 700 students each year. They take courses with 20 or fewer students that stimulate creativity and provoke in-depth discussion. Honors students also have opportunities to study abroad or take part in guided research.

WVU's commitment to students does not focus solely on the high achiever, however. The university supports all students by continually improving the libraries, providing learning centers, computer labs, a tutoring hotline, health services, a counseling center, a disabilities office, a career planning and placement center and an array of other student services.

To enhance campus life, the university also secures a wide range of entertainment —big-name concerts and lecturers, films, cultural events, art exhibits and special events such as Homecoming, Mountaineer Week (a tribute to Appalachian culture) and Parents Weekends. Many events such as the "Festival of Ideas" expose students to different cultures and ideas.

And, with approximately 250

The Personal Transit System (PRT) transports students between WVU's three Morgantown campuses.

student organizations flourishing, every student has a chance for extracurricular involvement.

Through service learning — a major WVU initiative — extracurricular and classroom learning become one. The Office of Service Learning Programs promotes opportunities for students to learn while helping others.

The university's Social Justice program ensures an environment of mutual respect that prepares students for living in a diverse world.

Living and learning

Since arriving at WVU in July 1995, President David C. Hardesty Jr. has stressed the importance of the student experience.

Revitalizing the freshman experience has been one of his most important initiatives. Operation Jump-Start fosters a sense of community by placing freshmen in residence halls according to similar majors and interests. Advising, entertainment and some classes take place in the residence halls, and faculty couples live on the premises to mentor students and help them make the most of their WVU experience.

WVU has also introduced a New Student Convocation to welcome freshmen and transfer

Celebrating potential and accomplishment: Graduation day.

WVU's rural health programs bring physicians to citizens of the state.

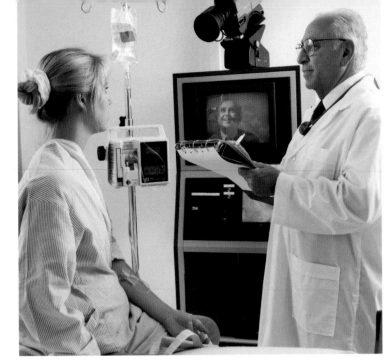

Mountaineer Doctor Television provides high-tech connections for visual and audio health care consultations via phone lines.

students to campus in the fall. The ceremony introduces new students to the university's academic opportunities. During the first week of classes, students enjoy three days of entertainment, including an outdoor concert during Fall Fest, an opportunity to celebrate the beginning of a new academic year.

The Mountaineer Parents Club is another student-centered initiative. Chapters connect parents with campus life and provide support and encouragement to students. The club has set up a toll-free helpline (1-800-WVU-0096) for parents to seek information or share compliments, suggestions and concerns. If a message is left, someone will respond within one business day if at all possible.

Creating new knowledge

Since its founding, WVU has functioned as the state's only research university. Funding from external sources exceeded $64 million in 1995-96.

WVU is a "Research I" institution; fewer than three percent of institutions classified by the Carnegie Foundation for the Advancement of Teaching earn that distinction. WVU is one of only 43 universities in the country that are designated as research

universities and also serve their states as land-grant institutions.

WVU's biggest research partner is the federal government. The university's relationship with the National Aeronautics and Space Administration (NASA) is an example of that partnership's benefits. WVU built NASA's $12 million Independent Verification and Validation facility with federal dollars. WVU faculty and staff conduct research at the center, which creates hundreds of private-sector jobs.

Faculty and students conducting major research projects work together with industry, other institutions and faculty in other departments, as well as the government. One example is another NASA project — building an unmanned airplane to survey environmental changes. This project unites faculty and students in the College of Engineering and Mineral Resources and the Eberly College of Arts and Sciences with those at Fairmont State College and Aurora Flight Sciences of West Virginia.

WVU centers that promote interdisciplinary research include the National Research Center for Coal and Energy, the Mary Babb Randolph Cancer Center, the Center for Women's Studies, the

A typical Big East football Saturday at Mountaineer Field is filled with excitement.

Concurrent Engineering Research Center, the Regional Research Center and the Harley O. Staggers National Transportation Center, among others.

Serving the state

Sharing WVU knowledge with state citizens is a major part of the land-grant mission. WVU's Extension Service alone reaches about 800,000 West Virginians through offices across the state. In addition to supporting agriculture, the service helps industry and provides families and children with many programs, including 4-H.

Students and health professionals at the Robert C. Byrd Health Sciences Center collaborate with state hospitals, clinics and local doctors toward one goal: a healthier West Virginia. The West Virginia Rural Health Initiative and the Kellogg Community Partnership program match medical, nursing, dental and pharmacy students with primary care sites in 36 counties.

Additionally, the Health Sciences Center provides outreach through MDTV, Mountaineer Doctor Television, a two-way video and audio communications network that enables specialist physicians at major medical centers to see and talk with patients at distant locations.

Service is not limited to

Extension and the Health Sciences, however. Every college and school shares its own expertise with state residents to make West Virginia's future brighter.

WVU sports

Whether it's the excitement of a football game at Mountaineer Field, the enthusiasm of a basketball game at the Coliseum or the determination of the national champion rifle team in the Shell Building rifle range, WVU is well-represented by its 20 varsity athletic programs and membership in the Big East all sports conference.

On autumn Saturdays, there is no more exciting place to be than Mountaineer Field, where the buckskin-clad Mountaineer mascot fires a rifle to the cheers of enthusiastic crowds. West Virginia football has participated in nine post-season bowl games during the past 15 years and met Notre Dame for the national championship in 1988 after a perfect regular season. In 1994, WVU had another perfect season and met Florida in the Sugar Bowl.

The Mountaineer men's Big East basketball program has enjoyed the same type of success, recording winning records in 17 of the past 18 seasons; the exciting Coliseum atmosphere has given WVU a home-court advantage that

has helped the Mountaineers to win more than 80 percent of the time since 1980.

The Mountaineer rifle team has won 11 of the last 13 NCAA national championships. Baseball won the 1996 Big East baseball title. Wrestling won two Eastern Wrestling League regular season championships and one tournament title during the '90s and has become a fixture in the Top 20 rankings. Gymnastics has qualified for 14 consecutive NCAA regionals and won the inaugural East Atlantic Gymnastics League title in 1996. During the past decade, Mountaineers have made 97 post-season trips to everything from bowl games to the NCAA finals.

Seating more than 14,000 for basketball games and able to host commencements, concerts and trade shows, the Coliseum is located on WVU's Evansdale Campus. Opened in 1970, the Coliseum is home to most of the Mountaineer athletic teams and houses many departmental offices and classrooms.

Mountaineer Field, home of 63,500 enthusiastic fans on football Saturdays, has established itself as one of the finest athletic facilities in the country. In addition to football, the men's and women's soccer teams play at Mountaineer Field.

WVU's 1995-96 Big East opener with Georgetown at the Coliseum was a sellout.

Information is available from the Office of Admissions and Records, PO Box 6009, West Virginia University, Morgantown, WV 26506-6009; or call toll free 1-800-344-WVU1, or visit WVU on the Web: http://www.wvu.edu; E-mail: wvuinfo@wvnvm.wvnet.edu Tours of WVU can be arranged by calling (304) 293-3489.

S·E·M Partners, Inc.

The young architects who founded Design Associates Architects - now S·E·M PARTNERS, Inc. - in 1959 were filled with hope and idealism of youth. They believed that if they really concentrated on their architecture - its bricks, its art, its people - that financial success would naturally follow. Life is never that simplistic,

but 37 years later their tenets for the fledgling firm - really serving clients, caring for employees, maintaining management continuity and always striving for quality design - have proven out. Founders Ralph Sounik and Ned B. Eller continue to direct a prosperous firm of thirty with projects ranging from residential remodeling to the recently completed $66 million Federal Prison in Beckley, West Virginia.

The firm first established a niche in residential, then religious design, and in 1965 finally secured

Federal Correctional Institute, Beckley

Elkins High School Library

its first school design commission for a small county district along the Ohio River. As educational design commissions became more numerous, the firm considered expanding from its office in Parkersburg, West Virginia.

That office first provided architectural services to Wood County Schools, one of the first "Better Schools Building Programs" in the state of West Virginia. Achievements in that county and the resulting references provided a successful foundation for school design commissions in a number of other counties in the state. This fueled the desire to expand in order to be able to serve West Virginia.

Many of S·E·M's clients continue to be educational institutions. However, the firm continues to diversify its client base. By relocating to Beckley in 1979, the firm expanded is geographic sphere and also its exposure to other project types. The office staff quickly became involved in local civic organizations as well as in the State Chapter of the AIA, and new types

PikeView High Computer Lab

of local commissions then began to come from that involvement - commercial and industrial projects, civic restorations, auto dealerships, condominiums, and health-care projects.

S·E·M's recent projects include

the Beckley Federal Correctional Institute (FCI) designed for the Federal Bureau of Prisons headquartered in Washington, D.C. This 567,000 SF Beckley FCI is designed to house 1,152 medium security inmates in the main facility and 384 minium security inmates in a satellite camp.

Other recent projects include several new high school facilities: the new $12 million Roane County High School was opened for the first school term in the fall of 1993, Elkins High School in Randolph County opened in December 1993, and PikeView High School in Mercer County was completed in the fall of 1994.

S·E·M is particularly proud of its award-winning Canyon Rim Visitors Center on the New River Gorge, completed in 1991; that successful project has led to ongoing work with the National Park Service. Another recent award for design excellence resulted in S·E·M's Exterior Restoration of Stewart Hall at West Virginia University.

Operating an architectural firm requires a balance of autonomy and unity. The four principals who serve West Virginia from the Beckley office are Ned Eller, David Beeman, Greg Eller and Blair Frier; all are members of the American Institute of Architects. Each handles a variety of responsibilities - whether design, project management, business development or construction administration.

Recently the firm has completed the design of several commercial and industrial projects. These projects have included the design of corporate offices, retail, banking and restaurant facilities, and medical office buildings. A sampling of industrial projects

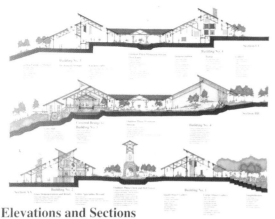

Elevations and Sections

Beckley Arts Center
West Virginia Parkways
Economic Development and Tourism Authority

S·E·M PARTNERS.

R.J.Ankrom
Associates

8

Canyon Rim Visitor Center

includes the design of facilities for the mining and petroleum industries, an international package delivery company and several maintenance facilities. Currently under construction is a vehicular maintenance facility for the West Virginia Parkways Economic Development and Tourism Authority.

High quality designs, responsive to client's needs, will always be a priority for S·E·M. The firm has consistently been recognized for design ability. The firm is fortunate to have received more awards for design from the West Virginia Chapter of The American Institute of Architects than any other firm. These projects are a collaborative effort between owner and architect and include awards for diverse project types including housing, historic restorations, museum and visitor information facilities, educational and commercial office facilities. Clients who place a high priority on design continue to choose S·E·M.

S·E·M PARTNERS, Inc. possess state of the art CADD technology. We realize the growing importance of computer aided design in today's architectural industry and utilize technological advances in our design process. Currently we use Sun Microsystems workstations with AutoCad, INTERGRAPH Microstation, and Sigma Design's ARRIS Architectural Design software operating on a UNIX platform. This configuration allows

Stewart Hall Exterior Restoration, WVU

tremendous flexibility with regard to other design programs and platforms. Currently S·E·M has eight Sun workstations which are totally networked. A project's database is accessible from any workstation. In addition, workstations are served by both an electrostatic plotter and a pen plotter. Additional workstations include both Apple PowerMac's and three DOS based machines. Additionally, workstations have the capability of running not only UNIX format of AutoCad, but also the DOS format.

Ned Eller attributes the firm's success to its professional capabilities as well as to its high level of client service. "We currently have a total of 13 registered architects. Each of those architects can successfully manage one or two projects simultaneously, thus giving us the ability to serve a number of major clients concurrently. Aggressive business development also helps," Eller adds. S·E·M sees a bright future. "We aren't afraid to work hard to achieve the goals we've set," Eller

College of Mineral and Energy Resources, WVU

says. Recently that hard work has paid off for S·E·M and the members of the firm believe that they can keep it that way.

S·E·M also provides architectural services to the states of Ohio, Michigan and Kentucky from its Columbus office.

One Valley Bank

One Valley Bank had its beginning two years after the end of the Civil War in a small room on Kanawha Street (now Kanawha Boulevard) near Summers Street in Charleston and has grown into a multi-bank holding company with 89 locations - 79 of which are in West Virginia and 10 in Virginia.

Six of the Valley's prominent citizens—aware of the need for adequate banking facilities in the midst of the reconstruction period following the war—obtained a bank charter on April 8,1867, subscribed $30,000 for capital stock and started **Kanawha Valley Bank**—the forerunner of One Valley Bancorp.

The six organizers included Levi J. Woodyard, the bank's first president; C.D. Reynolds; William Dickinson; Henry Clay Dickinson; John Q. Dickinson and Samuel Christy. Most of the original stockholders were or had been connected with the valley's salt industry.

ONE VALLEY BANK'S headquarters building, One Valley Square, in downtown Charleston.

STEVE LADISH

ONE VALLEY BANK®

Col. Henry C. Dickinson, Charles C. Lewis, William Dickinson, Col. John Q. Dickinson and his son, John L. Dickinson, served as presidents until 1949. Hayes Picklesimer held the office until 1967 when Hugh A. Curry took office. Curry was succeeded by Robert F. Baronner in 1975.

Baronner led the bank through an era of expansion and growth and fostered the formation of the bank holding company in 1982. He held the position of President & Chief Executive Officer of both the holding company and Kanawha Valley Bank.

In 1985 Baronner was succeeded as President & CEO of One Valley Bank in Charleston by J. Holmes Morrison as the bank's tenth chief executive officer. In 1991, when Baronner retired and became Chairman of the holding company's board of directors, Morrison was named President & CEO of One Valley Bancorp and Phyllis H. Arnold was named President & CEO of One Valley Bank in Charleston.

John L. Dickinson was the first Chairman of the bank's Board of Directors in 1949. He was followed by C.C. Dickinson, Hayes Picklesimer and Turner Ratrie, who was named Chairman in 1970 and served until his death in 1975.

The bank has occupied three buildings in downtown Charleston during its 129-year history. Following its initial location on Kanawha Street, the bank moved into the new Kanawha Valley Bank Building in 1929 at the corner of Capitol and Lee streets. After 57 years the bank moved to its present location, One Valley Square at Summers and Lee streets in 1976.

The location has not been the only change in past years. Total employees had grown to just over 300 by 1976. Twenty years later the total is over 2,100 with 814 employed in the flagship bank, One Valley Bank, N.A., located in Charleston.

In keeping with progressive changes in West Virginia banking laws, the holding company acquired several West Virginia banks as affiliates during the next few years with Kanawha Valley Bank in Charleston serving as the flagship bank. In 1987 the name of each affiliate bank was changed to **One Valley Bank**.

By June 30, 1996 One Valley Bancorp had twelve affiliate banks with $4.3 billion in total assets following the acquisition of CSB Financial Corporation, in Lynchburg, Virginia. CSB Financial, with ten locations, was renamed One Valley Bank of Central Virginia. It was the first out-of-state acquisition by West Virginia's largest bank holding company.

Today, the network of community banks provides a broad array of financial services to consumers, businesses and organizations. The bank also has a financial and trust services division, One Financial Place, and One Valley Securities Corporation, offering more sophisticated investors such products as mutual funds.

One Valley Bank's 79 West Virginia offices are located in 49 towns and cities including Beckley, Bluefield, Charleston, Clarksburg, Fairmont, Huntington, Martinsburg, Morgantown, Moundsville, Oak Hill, Parkersburg, Princeton, Ronceverte, Summersville, and Wheeling.

One Valley has a strong partnership feeling with the markets it serves not only to provide progressive financial services, but also to improve the lifestyle of our citizens, as well as enhance economic development.

J. Holmes Morrison, President & CEO of One Valley Bancorp, says, "As we act on our mission, we recognize our responsibility for stewardship in the communities we serve. We intend to act on that responsibility in the belief that it is not just good business, it is the right thing to do."

dedicated to retailing more West Virginia-made items. In all the travel plazas and the Princeton center, sales skyrocketed.

By 1994, Governor Gaston Caperton, a longtime proponent of the "West Virginia Made" label, began promoting the idea of putting the growing inventory of state-made items into other locations.

In a meeting with state park superintendents, Governor Caperton encouraged officials to stock park gift shops with West Virginia-made products. A new, quality line of locally made items replaced the imports of the past.

The idea for TAMARACK: *The Best of West Virginia* was born.

The Parkways Authority envisioned a place where West Virginia's very best could be showcased to the world, a place where visitors to the state could see first hand the remarkable history, heritage and talents West Virginia enjoys.

At the same time, the center would support thousands of West Virginians who honed their skills and talents in a variety of arts in small shops, in their homes, and in growing businesses.

The center would also be a location from which other West Virginia attractions could be promoted. As envisioned, visitors to the center are greeted as they walk through TAMARACK's doors by a staff ready to hand out information about whitewater rafting, skiing, resorts, camping, hiking, and other activities available in the region and in the state.

Ground for the center was broken in late summer 1994. TAMARACK opened its doors to the public in mid-May 1996.

Because of its location along the heavily traveled West Virginia Turnpike (Interstates 77 and 64), the center is expected to attract more than 500,000 visitors each year.

Joining TAMARACK

With nearly 1,200 artisans, craftspeople and food producers from each of the state's 55 counties already involved in the TAMA-RACK family, the Parkways Authority has not rested. Several times each year, jury sessions are held to find new products for the center.

No item is accepted for sale in TAMARACK until it has been

approved through the jury system. A panel of experts in the arts of pottery, woodworking, metal, textiles, glass and food come together to examine new crafts; equal review is given souvenir, manufactured and food items.

All those seeking entry into the TAMARACK market must be West Virginia residents. Individuals bringing samples of their work to the sessions find a dedicated panel of experts who appreciate the talents behind the products. The panel closely examines work samples, looking at the material used, the techniques employed and the appeal of the finished product.

If the work is accepted by the panel, the artisans meet next with TAMARACK buyers who help them ready the items for sale.

Because of the jury system, visitors find only the "**best**" of West Virginia on TAMARACK shelves.

More information

For more information about TAMARACK: *The Best of West Virginia*, write the center at One Tamarack Park, Beckley, WV 25801, or call 304-256-6843 or 1-88-TAMARACK.

Architect Clint Bryan.

Fenton Glass president Don Fenton with one of the vases his company makes which is available for sale at TAMARACK.

West Virginia Coal Association

Coal has a rich heritage in West Virginia and has contributed to the progress and well being of West Virginians since it was first discovered in what is now Boone County in 1759, more than a century before West Virginia became a state. The coal industry has played a major leadership role in the state's economic, political and social history. The industry has also been a center of controversy and the brunt of unfounded criticism, giving rise to battles in the arenas of labor,

environment and safety.

Over the years, West Virginia has furnished our nation and the world with the finest bituminous coal found anywhere. And today, West Virginia's coal miners apply efficient and effective mineral extraction technology that makes them the envy of their counterparts around the globe.

West Virginia exports more coal than any other state, has more longwall mining systems than any other state, leads the nation in underground coal production and sets the pace for the rest of the industry in reclamation and environmental protection. At the same time, the West Virginia coal industry exhibits a sense of responsibility - social, health, safety and environmental - that is unmatched anywhere in the world.

It was coal that transformed West Virginia from a frontier state to an industrial state. Coal in 62 recoverable seams can be found in 43 of the state's 55 counties. Knowledge of the coal reserves in western Virginia predated the American Revolution. Thomas Jefferson reported in his "Notes on the State of Virginia" that coal underlay most of the trans-Allegheny Ohio Valley. Jefferson's neighbor, John Peter Salling, traced huge deposits of bituminous coal along the Coal and Kanawha rivers in the mid-eighteenth century, but there was little demand for the mineral outside of local use in iron forges and blacksmith shops.

The first widespread use of West Virginia coal began when the saltworks along the Kanawha River expanded dramatically in the decades before the Civil War. Coal was used to heat the brine pumped from salt beds underneath the river. That modest use soon was dwarfed by the demands of a growing nation that looked to coal to heat its homes, power its factories and fuel its locomotives and steam-ships.

When the anthracite fields of Pennsylvania no longer could provide the tonnage needed, American industrialists discovered the massive coalfields of West Virginia. Large-scale investment soon opened the remote valleys along the New, Bluestone, Tug, Monongahela, and Guyandotte rivers. The Chesapeake & Ohio and Norfolk & Western railroads were built specifically to penetrate the rugged terrain of the coalfields, and investors purchased extensive tracts of land to lease to independent coal operators. Later, the Virginian and the Baltimore & Ohio also became coal-hauling lines as well.

In those days, coal mining was highly labor intensive, but only a few rugged mountaineers lived in the remote, isolated hills and hollows where the operations developed. Thus, operators recruited much of their labor from two human migrations underway around 1900. Thousands of African-Americans fleeing discrimination and segregation left the Deep South, and many exchanged the poverty of the cotton fields for the bustling coalfields. Meanwhile, European immigrants fleeing religious persecution and impending war came to America to find jobs and homes, and many came from coal-bearing regions of Europe to the prosperous mines in West Virginia.

Over the next half century, tonnage and employment increased dramatically. By 1950, some 125,000 West Virginia coal miners lived and worked in more than 500 company towns built to house them and their families. Whole new cities sprang up where silent mountains had rested for centuries.

Although coal mining was dark, dirty and inherently danger-ous, many miners enjoyed their day's work. They enjoyed being skilled craftsmen who produced a product they could take pride in. People liked the close friendly life in the company towns, where ties of family, neighbors, church, school and home bred a close-knit

community. Old-timers fondly recall company baseball teams, neighborhood gatherings, church suppers and other characteristic features of coalfield life. Today many decry conditions in the "coal camps," but miners and their families fared as well as most working-class Americans of that era, and better than those unfortunate souls who labored in urban sweatshops or as rural sharecroppers.

West Virginia's coalfields were home to some of the most significant labor strife in this nation's history, as the United Mine Workers battled coal operators for control of the industry. Spectacular incidents such as the famed Matewan Massacre and the Battle of Blair Mountain, landmarks in American labor history, showed the strategic importance of the state's crucial industry, and its national significance.

After World War II, coal mining became increasingly dependent upon mechanization and sophisticated machinery. Continuous mining machines, conveyor belts and other advances increased tonnage dramatically. Surface mining operations and longwall machines produced astounding outputs in an efficient and safe manner. Increased productivity meant more coal could be produced by fewer miners. Pointing to that lower level of employment, some foolishly argue that coal's day is over. They couldn't be more wrong.

Today, West Virginia's coal industry contains more than 500 companies, provides more than 30,000 direct jobs, pays $1 billion dollars in annual payroll and hundreds of million dollars to state and local governments in taxes and contributions. Coal is still the rock-solid backbone of West Virginia's industrial economy.

Since its inception in 1915, the West Virginia Coal Association has been the voice of the state's coal industry, making sure that West Virginia coal continues to be the "Fuel of Choice" for the entire world. Coal is West Virginia!

Current Association Members:
AEP
AMVEST Minerals Groups, Inc.
Arch of West Virginia
Battle Ridge Companies
Bethlehem Mines Corporation
Bluestone Coal Corp.
Brooks Run Coal Company
Burco Resources Corp.
Catenary Coal Co.
Coal Power Corp.
CONSOL Inc.
Cyprus Amax
Eastern Associated Coal Corp
Hobet Mining, Inc.
Imperial/Milburn Collieries
International Resources, Inc.
Mountaineer Coal Development Co.
Massey Coal Services, Inc.
MAXIM Management Co.
Mingo Logan Coal Company
Northland Resources Company
Pen Coal Corporation
The Pittston Coal Group
Roblee Coal Company
U. S. Steel Mining Co., Inc.
Virginia Crews Coal Company
Westmoreland Coal Company
Zeigler Coal Holding

State College System of West Virginia

Dr. Clifford M. Trump, Chancellor

The State College System recognizes that West Virginia's future and West Virginia's economy are inextricably linked to the effectiveness of its educational system. In the next century, the strength of the nation and the state of West Virginia will depend upon the skills, industriousness, quality orientation, and trained intelligence of the workforce. Strengthening state and national competitive advantage will require that business, industry, government, and higher education move toward cooperative endeavors in order to use limited resources most efficiently and effectively.

The State College System of West Virginia has taken the task of developing a plan that will carry West Virginia's nine state colleges successfully into the twenty-first century.

Established in 1989, the State College System of West Virginia is comprised of seven four-year colleges and two free-standing community colleges. The State College System is governed by a sixteen-member Board of Directors, consisting of ten citizens appointed by the governor; three ex-officio members; and an elected representative from each of the advisory councils of students, faculty, and classified staff. The chancellor serves as chief ex-ecutive officer for the system, with the presidents as chief executive officers for the institutions. The presidents report to the board through the chancellor.

The board and chancellor receive advice and recommendations on system issues from the presidents, the Central Office staff, and from system-wide staff, student, and faculty advisory councils. Each president receives in-put on campus matters from a Board of Advisors and from a variety of organizations representing the institution's faculty, classified staff, students, alumni, and other interested parties.

The mission of the State College System of West Virginia is to provide instruction, scholarly activities, and service that are high in quality, cost-effective, and accessible to the citizens of the state.

Bluefield State College

Entering its second century of academic excellence, Bluefield State College is positioned to look back on a very strong past and, at the same time, stand ready for the challenges and opportunities in its future.

With 12 nationally accredited programs of study, Bluefield State College is attuned to the needs of this region's businesses and industry. Additionally, the college's Center for International Understanding fosters global cooperation in higher education and industry. With both associate and baccalaureate degree programs, BSC has designed a seamless curriculum approach to enable students receiving a two-year degree to move easily and with full academic credit into a four-year program.

Students relax at Mahood Circle

Enrollment at BSC has grown significantly over the past 20 years, with an 88% rise in enrollment since 1975. There has been a 24% increase in first-time freshmen since 1990. Significantly, 12 of every 13 students attending BSC in 1995 were West Virginia residents.

In 1994-95, the number of institutional scholarships increased 38% over the prior year's awards.

BSC has 13 computer laboratories and 380 computers dedicated to student use. Additionally, Bluefield State College has built a site-of-origination television studio on its main campus and will begin utilizing a microwave instructional technology network to Lewisburg and Beckley during the 1996-97 academic year.

The college is also experiencing significant growth at its off-campus sites in Lewisburg, Beckley and Welch. Plans call for Bluefield State's Greenbrier Community College Center to relocate in 1997 into the historically-significant downtown Lewisburg facility formerly housing the Greenbrier College for Women. The Beckley Center of BSC has enjoyed enrollment and service growth since moving into its new facility in the Harper Industrial Park.

Bluefield State College's Community and Technical College has signed agreements of understanding with other institutions of higher education to coordinate community and technical college academic offerings in McDowell and Raleigh Counties.

The college has taken a proactive role in offering customized training programs for workforce enhancement at several area businesses and has entered into partnerships with several agencies to coordinate and increase the efficiency of instruction to students.

Now Internet-accessible (http://www.bluefield.wvnet.edu/), Bluefield State College offers affordable, accessible, and relevant higher education to equip our students for the opportunities of the 21st century.

LOCATION: Athens, Mercer County, a community of 1,000. The Beckley Concord Center serves Raleigh and adjacent counties.
PHONE: (304) 384-3115.
FAX: (304) 384-9044.
E-MAIL: PRENM@CCVMS.WVNE
T.EDU
P.O. Box 1000, Athens, WV 24712

Concord College

One-hundred-twenty-five years ago the people of rural southern West Virginia joined the movement to bring higher education to all parts of the Mountain State in the form of teacher training schools. "Fine," said state government, "as long as you find the land and pay to build it."

The citizens acquired six acres of land in Concord and raised the funds to open Concord State Normal School. When fire devastated the downtown site in 1910, the people rallied once more and raised enough money to buy 26 acres for a new campus and building, which are still in use today.

Times have changed. The town is now Athens, renamed because it was a center for learning. The name of the institution has reflected its continuous expansion, becoming Concord State Teachers College in 1931 and, finally, Concord College in 1943. Over the years the curriculum has evolved to include business, and other course offerings. In recent years thriving programs in social work, travel industry management, and pre-professional fields have been nurtured.

A proud member of the State College System, Concord is the only residential public college south of Charleston and cooperates with Bluefield State College and community colleges to provide maximum student access and cost-effective services. The Center for Economic Action at Concord has been helping the region's businesses since 1963. The Beckley Concord College Center has been serving new populations since 1991. Concord's mission also includes a longstanding commitment to public service; it is the only public institution in the nationwide Bonner Scholars network, in which thousands of students earn money for college by helping improve their communities.

Fairmont State College

Fairmont State College, founded in 1867, is the largest four-year, state-supported institution in West Virginia, with a student enrollment in excess of 6,500. FSC is located in Fairmont, in the north central part of the state. Most students are state residents and there are slightly more women than men.

FSC's 80-acre campus has 13 major buildings; there is also a Clarksburg campus, various satellite facilities across the region, and the Robert C. Byrd National Aerospace Education Center in Bridgeport.

Students living on campus are housed in three residence halls and take their meals at the centrally located dining hall or at the popular "Nickel" food court in the student center. For students living off-campus, private accommodations border the college.

FSC's Child Care Center provides for children while parents are in class. The Feaster Center athletic complex offers facilities for swimming, racquetball, and basketball. Newman Center and Wesley Foundation are available to help meet the spiritual needs of students.

FSC has a long and storied athletic tradition. As a member of the NCAA Division II, FSC has athletic teams in baseball, basketball, cheerleading, cross- country, football, golf, softball, swimming, tennis, and volleyball. There is also an extensive and well-organized intramural program.

FSC offers one-year certificates, two-year associate degrees, and four-year bachelor's degrees, as well as a wide range of continuing education classes. FSC offers courses of study leading to baccalaureate degrees in the humanities, social and natural sciences, teacher education, business, industrial technology, and the fine arts.

Fairmont State College offers 166 program areas in the following divisions: business and economics; education/health, physical education, recreation, and safety; fine arts; language and literature; science, mathematics, and health careers; social science; technology; and family and consumer sciences. FSC has more than 200 full-time faculty members.

For more information, phone toll-free (800) 641- 5678.

Hardway Hall

Glenville State College

The Clock Tower

In 1872, Glenville State College began as the "Glenville Branch of the State Normal School of West Virginia." Although the primary purpose in establishing Glenville Normal was to educate teachers, preparatory courses for college were also authorized. At different times, this curriculum was designated as "Classical," "Scientific," or "Academic." In 1930, Glenville State Normal School was given college status. The first Bachelor of Arts degrees were granted in 1931 to a class of nine, eight of whom were men!

Glenville State is the most centrally located of all colleges in West Virginia. Its rural location may suggest isolation, but with Interstate 79 only 15 miles away, Glenville becomes easily accessible to the outside world. It takes only one trip to Glenville to see how the town's beauty inspired our state song, "The West Virginia Hills!" The college reposes among soft rambling hillsides and quietly rushing rivers. Not only is Glenville State College the ideal place for an education, but the town and surrounding areas are full of history, beauty, and activities that put you in the center of it all.

Shepherd College

Shepherd College is located in historic Shepherdstown just 70 miles from the nation's capital. The college's location provides the student with the best of both worlds: a pastoral campus of gently rolling hills in a small town setting, combined with access to the cultural and educational opportunities that the metropolitan area provides. Shepherd's 323-acre campus sits atop the bluffs overlooking the Potomac River.

Founded in 1871, Shepherd College is a public, liberal arts college that enjoys an outstanding reputation: the college is profiled in *Barron's Three Hundred Best Buys in College Education* and, for 12 consecutive years, has been the only West Virginia college selected for listing in *Peterson's Guide to Competitive Colleges*.

The college's 3,700 students have the choice of more than 70 programs of study including bachelor's degree programs and pre-professional studies through the college and two-year associate's degrees through Shepherd's Community and Technical College component.

Shepherd's close proximity to Washington, D.C., led to the development of the Washington Gateway Program, which allows

McMurran Hall

students to take advantage of the wealth of cultural resources and educational opportunities available in the metro area.

Shepherd College is also the home of the Institute of International Training, Trade, and Development, a training program for top Russian senior government officials and industrial managers; the George Tyler Moore Center for the Study of the Civil War, which is developing a database of military, socio-economic, and medical data on Union and Confederate soldiers, sailors, and marines; and the Contemporary American Theater Festival, dedicated to producing works by new and emerging playwrights and to cutting-edge theater.

Southern West Virginia Community College was established as an open door comprehensive community college on July 1, 1971, by combining two existing branches of Marshall University. Both the Williamson and Logan branches had been in operation since 1963 under the academic, fiscal, and administrative control of Marshall University, providing primarily the first two years of liberal arts, teacher education, and career programs in secretarial science and radiologic technology.

The college's first permanent building was dedicated in Williamson in 1971. From 1971 to 1974, Southern expanded its program offerings and enlarged its community service offerings. In 1974, the college expanded its operation to many off-campus sites in Mingo, Logan and Wyoming counties. This expansion continued until 1976 when the West Virginia Board of Regents established informal service boundaries for all the state's public colleges and universities. Southern was assigned a service area of 1,900 square miles to provide undergraduate education and community service.

In 1975, facilities were acquired in Wyoming County; in 1977, the Boone County Center was estab-lished; and in 1979, a permanent campus was dedicated in Logan.

As the student population increased, the need for larger facilities became evident. In 1982, the Southern Foundation purchased a building in Madison to house the Boone County Center. In 1983, the Board of Regents purchased the facility from the foundation for $190,000. Renovation, totaling $384,498, was completed in 1987.

In 1986, property was purchased at Saulsville for the new site of the Wyoming County Center. Construction began in January 1989, and was completed in December 1989 at a cost of $1,963,035.

In 1988, a new multi-purpose addition was added to the Logan Campus at a cost of $3,166,155.

In 1981, the college expanded its service area when, by interstate agreement, students from Martin and Pike Counties in Kentucky were permitted to attend Southern at in-state fees.

In 1995, Southern expanded its service area again to serve citizens in Lincoln ans McDowell Counties.

In 1996, through SBA funding, State College System Board of Directors and institutional funds, Southern will construct a new campus in Boone County, adjacent to the Boone Career and Technical Center, where programs and services will be shared by both institutions. Classes are expected to begin in the new facility during the Fall 1997 semester.

Southern provides an enjoyable learning atmosphere for a population of approximately 3,000 students.

Southern provides students with the most up-to-date technology. A new electronic interactive classroom system connects five college locations with two-way audio and video.

West Liberty State College

On March 30, 1837, the Virginia legislature granted a charter to establish an academy at West Liberty. A year later, in the home of Rev. Nathan Shotwell, the first class met. The school remained a private, coeducational institution, providing a classical education until March 1, 1870, when it became a part of West Virginia's higher education system. For the following 61 years, it served as a normal school, training students "in the arts of the teacher."

In 1931, under the leadership of President John S. Bonar, the institution became West Liberty State Teachers College and granted its first baccalaureate degrees. In 1943, the school became West President Paul Elbin from 1935 to 1970, West Liberty State College evolved into its current status.

Today, West Liberty is known for its high caliber of education, excellent quality of student life, superb setting and affordability. As a regional, multifaceted college it offers curricula in the liberal arts, business, education, the sciences and health professions.

A most striking element of the campus is its sheer beauty. Built around a sprawling quadrangle and nestled in the hills of Northern West Virginia, the setting is rural, yet is only an hour from Pittsburgh and just minutes from Wheeling and Oglebay Park.

The campus features a state-of-the-art library, a recreational and athletic facilities, and a new science building. Dormitories present a variety of options, including coed floors, apartments and traditional offerings.

Individual attention is among West Liberty's hallmarks. The faculty is overwhelmingly full-time, seasoned and primarily concerned with students' education. With its high- technology computer labs in science, music and graphic arts, WLSC steps boldly into the next millennia, bringing with it a long tradition of quality.

Main Hall

West Virginia Northern Community College

West Virginia Northern Community College responds to the increasing demands of business and industry for innovative programs, such as workplace literacy and contracted instruction, along with other types of partnerships and community services that promote cultural, economic and environmental development and awareness. Known as a leader in its use of instructional technologies, Northern prepares learners for the demands of a rapidly changing, increasingly complex, and technologically sophisticated world.

West Virginia Northern offers both certificate and associate degree programs. Credit courses lead to associate degrees designed for transfer to four-year colleges and universities as well as associate degrees for immediate entry into a job. In addition, developmental and community education courses are offered.

With course offerings at a variety of sites as well as flexible scheduling of classes, Northern accommodates students with full-time and part-time jobs as well as those with family responsibilities.

Campuses are located in New Martinsville, Weirton, and Wheeling, serving Brooke, Hancock, Marshall, Ohio, Tyler, and Wetzel counties, as well as enrolling students from adjacent areas of eastern Ohio and western Pennsylvania.

Dr. Linda S. Dunn
President

Students:
undergraduate: 2,921
women: 2,011
men: 910

Students receiving financial aid:
46%

West Virginia Northern Community College
1704 Market Street
Wheeling, WV 26003
(304) 233-5900

New Martinsville (304) 455-4685
Weirton (304) 723-2210

West Virginia State College

West Virginia State College is centrally located in the Kanawha Valley, the hub of government, culture, and business in the state. Founded in 1891 as an institution of higher learning for black Americans, the college is one of two land-grant colleges in West Virginia. It was first accredited by the North Central Association of Colleges and Schools in 1927, making it the first of the 1890 land-grant colleges and the first college in West Virginia to earn the distinction that continues to this day.

Situated on a modern, 83 acre, beautifully landscaped campus, West Virginia State College offers easy accessibility. A fully automated library and modern science building are among the facilities equipped to provide the latest in technology, instruction and research facilities. The college offers 17 baccalaureate and 20 associate degree programs. Special accreditations in chemistry, teacher education, nuclear medicine technology, recreation service, social work, and electronics technology demonstrate excellence in these disciplines.

As a nationally proclaimed "Living Laboratory of Human Relations," West Virginia State College takes great pride in the diversity of its faculty, staff and student body. Reasonable tuition and fees offer attainable higher education for the citizens of West Virginia and the Kanawha Valley.

Hamblin Hall

St. Mary's Hospital

St. Mary's Hospital's tradition of compassionate caring began on November 6, 1924, when eight Pallottine Missionary Sisters opened a 35-bed hospital. Through their motto "The Love of Christ Impels Us," these pioneer Sisters created a strong foundation by their dedication and hard work.

St. Mary's growth was rapid.

In 1926, 376 patients were admitted with 59 physicians on staff. St. Mary's School of Nursing opened in 1929 and a new nursing school was built in 1947.

In 1965, the region's first radiation therapy center for cancer treatment and the area's only cardiac intensive care unit were established.

In 1976, St. Mary's affiliated with Marshall University School of Medicine. The bed count, as today, remains 440.

The first full body Computerized Tomography Unit was installed in 1977. In 1979, the cardiac catheterization lab and two open-heart operating rooms opened.

In 1980, St. Mary's became a Regional Cancer Center by installing a linear accelerator in Radiation Oncology.

In 1987, St. Mary's implemented a joint MRI Unit. A nuclear cardiology department and angioplasty service also were opened.

In 1988, St. Mary's began the nation's first joint Level II trauma service.

Today with 300 staff physicians, St. Mary's provides advanced treatment in cardiac care, cancer treatment, women's health, emergency/trauma services and psychiatric service.

St. Mary's Regional Heart Center performs more than 550 open heart surgeries annually and offers interventional cardiology services, non-invasive cardiology testing and nuclear cardiology studies.

Accredited by the American College of Surgeons since 1957, St. Mary's Regional Cancer Center provides experienced cancer care. It is supported through research and education by Duke Comprehensive Cancer Center. Duke's support services include a sharing of clinical research protocols and consultation between local physicians and Duke's nationally recognized experts.

St. Mary's Women's Health Services features "Women's Care," a designated unit for female medical/surgical patients. In the Obstetrical Unit, a mother may labor, deliver, recover and have her post-partum stay in a private suite. A Level II Neonatal Care Nursery and two surgical suites (for caesareans) are also located there.

As a Level II Trauma Center, St. Mary's treats and rehabilitates the critically injured through comprehensive surgical/medical specialties.

The Surgical, Medical and Coronary intensive care units serve the critically ill/injured. St. Mary's specialized units provide advanced care for patients requiring neurosurgical/neurological or orthopedic procedures.

St. Mary's Psychiatric Service treatment programs for adults and adolescents include the Adult Psychiatric Unit, Substance Abuse Unit and Adolescent Treatment Unit, and the Partial Hospitalization Program.

St. Mary's is the largest hospital in the Tri-State, Cabell County's largest private employer and the second-largest medical facility in West Virginia.

As a teaching facility, St. Mary's trains medical residents and is home to St. Mary's School of Radiologic Technology and the School of Nursing.

St. Mary's Outpatient Center is scheduled for completion in July 1997. This $17 million, 74,000 square foot building will house physicians and outpatient services.

St. Mary's commitment to the finest care continues. We face the future with the same determination and dedication of our founding Sisters.

Afterword

West Virginia: Mountain Majesty is a history book about the future. The Mountain State has long veiled its heritage in mystery. A state baptized, nurtured, and matured in conflict, we have avoided questions about our past, fearful that ancient animosities could rekindle in the light of revelation.

As a frontier, the French and Indian War bloodied our Allegheny borders. The Civil War divided families and severed our political fortunes from the Old Dominion. In the labor wars early in this century, our forefathers fought over strongly held beliefs in the tumultuous relationship of capital and labor, between employer and employee, between owner and worker.

So when a West Virginian is faced with the question, "which side were you on," it can become personal, accusatory and a source of discomfort. But looking to our history for guidance to the future makes sense. Our cultural heritage is a rich resource for historians and for travelers enjoying our natural beauty.

The partnership between cultural resources and the business enterprises they support, and by which they are supported, is the future for West Virginia. This book highlights that partnership, and is a product of it. What has worked for those businesses profiled in these pages will work for future businesses attracted by our traditions and our family-oriented quality of life.

West Virginia: Mountain Majesty is a book about these traditions and our proud heritage — all the things we cherish most about ourselves. As we share these traditions with our visitors, we can take pride in the fierce, independent spirit resonating in our state's motto "Montani Semper Liberi," Mountaineers Always Free. Working with those businesses who share in that pride and independence, the Division of Culture and History provides a solid foundation for a future built on our past.

Let me just take a moment to acknowledge the work of two men without whom this publication would never have come to be. Mike Perry, CEO Banc One of West Virginia, saw in this project the opportunity to promote the marriage of cultural and commercial traditions. He believes strongly in this marriage and its economic development potential, and he worked diligently to convince others in the business community of its value. Without his vision and enthusiasm, the book would have lost heart and died.

Ken Sullivan, the editor of *Goldenseal* magazine, was the focus for all the creative work done on the project. He coordinated the assignments, worked with printing companies and archives, oversaw the photographs, copy, layout and design, and stood staunchly by the project from start to finish. The quality of the final product is testament to his vision and professionalism.

And finally, to the people of West Virginia, I raise this praise: You are what this is all about — your past, your future, your spirit enfolded in Mountain Majesty — West Virginia.

Bill Drennen
Commissioner,
Division of Culture and History

GERALD S. RATLIFF

The *West Virginia: Mountain Majesty* photographers:

Ann Beattie
Larry Belcher
Brian Blauser
Bill Farrar
David E. Fattaleh
Mel Grubb
Todd A. Hanson
Greg Henshall
Michael Keller
George J. Kossuth
Rick Lee
Steve Payne
Peggy Powell
Larry Pierce
Gerald S. Ratliff
Stephen J. Shaluta, Jr.
Van Slider
Ron Snow

A special thanks to the unknown photographers from long ago, whose pictures we have taken from the West Virginia State Archives, from the West Virginia and Regional History Collection at West Virginia University, and from the files of *Goldenseal*, the magazine of West Virginia traditional life.

GERALD S. RATLIFF